Paradise
in
Indonesia
South China Sea Isles up close

compiled by Bob Godsey
edited by Madelyn Godsey

PublishAmerica

Hardcover 978-1-4626-1780-7
Softcover 978-1-4626-1781-4
PUBLISHED BY PUBLISHAMERICA, LLLP
www.publishamerica.com
Baltimore

Printed in the United States of America

Acknowledgement

Thanks to Mr. George Hampe, of Bremen, Indiana, who made these journals available. The journals span the years 1931-1936. They are historically and culturally revealing. They reveal an intimate contact with the common citizens caught in a world wide economic depression.

Prelude

In 1931, Mr. Hampe's sister, Tonia Rose Gale, and her first husband Joseph Rosenberg a.k.a. Rose, ventured forth without benefit of tour guide or interpreters. Their journey was most unusual in that they traveled deck class, fourth class, bus, ox cart, and horse back and on foot. They used no interpreter or tour guide. They were true vagabonds.

We are grateful for the opportunity to edit this set of seventeen journals together with accompanying letters, and photos. The journal entries are revised and edited to avoid redundancy and to provide clarity where appropriate. Redundancy occured most often when Joe and Tonia wrote in the same journal.

The reader will be enlightened by the historical significance of this time in which they traveled in Sumatra and the islands of South China Sea.

Our first volume, "On Our Own in the Far East," revealed their adventures in Japan, China, and the Philippines. With that behind them we now travel with them into the South China Sea.

Itinerary

Foreword

Japan and China were now behind them; the Vagabond Couple had been exposed to unspeakable conditions of poverty, but awed by the splendor of the ancient cultures of Japan and China. They witnessed Japanese and Chinese people striving to assimilate western ideas while at the same time holding true to their unique age-old culture. Joe and Tonia made many friends along the way as they learned how to cope and better appreciate their experiences.

Joe and Tonia traveled during a time when major changes were taking place in the decade before World War II as the seeds of war were being sown. They observed and listened, and interacted with the common people. They reported the details of their adventures to their family, and to their California friend, Patrick O'Day.

The first volume of this work began with a letter written to Patrick O'Day in which Joe explained their reasoning for undertaking this wild plan to travel around the world. They started their journey in August 19, 1931, from California. We begin with an excerpt from the letter Joe wrote to Patrick. —-August, 1931

Dear Patrick,

Will this startle you, or did you have an inkling that I would spring this news on you one of these days? We are off to the strange lands on the other side of the globe for a few years. We feel we cannot keep on postponing our cherished trip any longer. You know how Tonia has been nurturing for years the picture of herself roaming about in the glamorous Far East. Well, she is now ready to run off by herself if I don't close up my desk and go with her.

All jests aside, for the last six months I have been questioning myself whether I was not making the same mistake as thousands of others before me have done— of waiting until I accumulate enough money so that I might travel in great comfort. Most probably, I will never become rich, and if I did, it may be too late. I may be too old by that time and not even have the same interests and urges as now. When my uncle, who is close to sixty, returned from a "conducted" round-the-world tour two years ago, he related to me the remark made to him by a native guide in Java: "Don't you have any young people in your country at all?"

Patrick, I want to travel while I am still young and can thoroughly enjoy it and while hardships and adventurous exploits hold no fear for me. I do not want to wait until I might have to give over my keeping into the hands of Cook's Travel Agency and be guided and led about wearing smoked glasses and carrying a cane.

It's true I can count only twenty-eight years - and Tonia three years less - the very age when people are supposed to be filled with hopes and desires of building a future and establishing themselves in their communities. But, we must be vagabonds, for I don't know of any desire which is stronger in either of us than that of first, getting away from our sophisticated and altogether too-complicated life, and then, seeing and studying the lives of strange and far-away peoples.

What are a few years in one's life? They fly by pretty fast anyway and usually unnoticed at that. Tell me, what could we lose by saying good-bye to this worried world for a while? I am sure that my share of troubles will patiently wait for me until I return, so why be anxious to cope and grapple with them now? Let's play "hooky" and have a holiday!

We have a little money now, and we are going to see how far we can make it stretch. We intend to be gone for three years. Although we kept it all from you, we spent time on the ranch carefully studying the countries we are about to visit, so that we may be free and never have to be depend on guides. I am lucky that Tonia is a fine climber and a sport who is not afraid of hardship. If we get stranded, leave it to her to make the most of it. Do these names sound as alluring to your ears as to ours — Japan, China, Cochin-China, Cambodia, the Dutch East Indies, Siam, Burma, the great land of India, Kashmir, remote Afghanistan and Persia, Mesopotamia, and the Near East?

Another thing, for years a dream of mine has been to learn more about the art of wood-carving in China and Kashmir. On this journey we will take time for that and perhaps for Indian sandal- making so that I'll be able to make you a pair when I come home. There are the Javanese secrets of batik and dyeing that Tonia wants to know about, and then, there is weaving too. There is going to be so much to learn on the Oriental holiday! You know how we have always been two "collecting mad-caps," browsing in dusty corners, and finding those beloved bits of Chinese, or Indian, or Japanese art that have always puzzled us as to their exact origin. Well, now we are going to find the source of those beautiful objects. And what about the different dances and theaters and festivals that we will see with our own eyes, and the strange, unfamiliar dishes that we will taste? Pat, I feel that these years we are taking off are going to be the richest period in our whole lives!

Now, here is a promise. From each and every country you will hear from us, how we are faring, and what we are experiencing, and also how inexpensively we can travel. And should it turn out to be feasible to roam around-the-world on one dollar and a half per day for the each of us, including every expense, then there will certainly be a next time, and you'll have to come along with us. The gods, you know, are very reluctant in doling out riches. They have their favored few, and that is all.—

Regards, Joe and Tonia

Singapore

After seeing Manila and taking in its cultural mix, we sailed back to Hong Kong. There we made ready to continue our adventure in the South China Sea. We sailed from Hong Kong to Singapore which is considered the most cosmopolitan city in the world with every Asian race east of Suez represented there. Singapore, under British rule, has only about ten-thousand Europeans; the majority is Chinese.

Three-and-a-half months ago, we started on our wild adventure absorbing the wonders of Hawaii, Japan, and China, the dust storms and heat, and the smells of Peking, visiting Buddhist temples, the Great Wall of China, and Americanized Manila. We have been treated warmly, as family, by new friends. All has been an exhilarating shock to our senses. It has immersed us in ancient cultures, and exposed us to current conditions which are beyond our imagination. It has broadened us beyond our expectations. And now, we are moving into equatorial waters of the South China Sea. With us now are two young men (Kane and Lee) whom we met in Hong Kong. They too are heading for Java, Bali, and French Indo-China. With Java and Bali ahead of us in the next few weeks, our spirits are high. We are filled with confidence and expectation. We will continue to keep in touch with you and family.

December 25, 1931
Dear Everyone,
Merry Christmas! We are on board again on our N.Y.K. Liner, Suwa Maru, which will pull out for Singapore at sunrise tomorrow or earlier. We are traveling through Java and Bali and Indo China with two congenial American

boys, Lee and Kane. We are leaving baggage and going with only a knapsack. It's going to be great fun!

Our neat little "Suwa Maru," looks quite insignificant alongside two newer and larger Ocean Liners. It is an old ship but is spick and span as are all the Japanese liners. Since we want to be in Singapore for New Years, we can't wait for a bigger liner. The Suwa Maru serves us just fine… Regards, Joe and Tonia

Singapore, "The Lion City"
January 2, 1932
Well, we landed in this famous port of the East, and it was lovely. We stayed only a few days, but our friends whom we met in L.A. and Mr. Levison's daughter, who now lives here, treated us royally.

The vegetation was wondrous. Monkeys jumped around in the gardens, and the medley of faces here were astounding! There were Chinese, Japanese, Burmese, Malays, and Indians of every color and description— Sikhs, Parsees, and Tamils, who were as coal black as natives that came from Ceylon. The costumes ranged from g-strings and loin cloths to brilliant sarongs wrapped like skirts. The men wore skirts and had long hair. It seemed to us that every culture in the East was represented here. I doubt we could see this variety in any other city. We at home heard of how terrible a place is Singapore, and how hot and godforsaken it is. But, we found it to be lovely! Soft breezes blow, and it is not too hot. The vegetation was far lovelier than in Manila, and the diversity makes it a fascinating place.

*****

Singapore is a small island on the south tip of the Malay Peninsula. The peninsula has two million acres in rubber plantations which supplies three-fourths of the world's rubber. The Dutch contract their

native labor through the Japanese for growing and harvesting great quantities of coconut copra, pepper, sugar, tapioca and sago. There are, also, the richest tin mines in the world and half the world's tea.

It was a center for private business one hundred years ago. Sir Raffles, representing the British East India Company, dealt with the Sultan of Jahore. Fabulous fortunes were made through this trade until his death at age forty-five, and his estate in England was confiscated.

*****

Malay's people seemed relaxed. They had little patience for extensive farming for they lived from hand to mouth and worked only when their meager funds were gone. Foreigners used Malays mostly as gardeners and chauffeurs as they were known to be dependable and steady drivers. The Chinese did most of the farming, and most of the household servants are Chinese who were reported to be good and fast workers. They worked mainly on rubber plantations as they were the cheapest labor in the orient receiving thirty cents per day for tapping rubber trees. The women, however, received only twenty-five cents per day which was barely enough to keep them alive. The young Chinese coolies seemed to be the only ones who could stand the heat, but they got played out after a few years, so there was always an influx of new coolies coming into Malaysia. The Chinese who were born there however were never coolies. They took office jobs. The common language for all these inhabitants was a simplified Malay, or pidgin Malay. The Malays, mostly Mohammedan, were small people resembling Filipinos and were like drone bees in that they do not work. They were a happy-looking people. Some of the women were beautiful, wore silver bracelets and anklets with colorful sarong skirts and tight blouses. Only rich Malayans practiced polygamy now. They married young but did not have large families (usually fewer than three children.) They lived in small bamboo and palm huts and slept on woven-mats. Most of them chewed betel nuts which are supposed to take away fatigue and hunger. The rolled up leaf is spread with a mixture of lime, ground nuts and other ingredients and chewed. It produces blood red spittle which blackens the teeth and swells the tongue and lips. The natives took tobacco and rubbed it over their teeth to remove betel stain.

Opium-smoking was licensed in Singapore, and fortunes were made from it. The opium stores were owned by the British government and guarded by soldiers. The stores looked like prisons with iron bars. The government tried to ban new smokers but people came anyway to get their rations. There is an Opium League which sets the rules, but this practice has been a disgrace to the British administration.

The Malay Peninsula is divided into five states ruled by native sultans and counseled by British advisors. The port of Singapore is a lively city with many fabulous millionaires. It was built to compete with neighboring Dutch colonies. *Mammon*, or money, is supreme here. By boat, it is two days away from Java and four days from Siam. There were few points of interest in this city, but native life and the variety of races supplied a never-ending panorama of color. Besides the Chinese, Japanese, and Malays, there were also Persians, Arabs, Jews, Armenians, and Hindus of many castes, Parses, Sikhs from Bengal, Tamils from Ceylon, and many others, all presenting shades of colors of skin and a riot of costumes. We saw brilliant magenta, red, or blue spots between the eyes on many Hindus which were their caste marks. Some had white smeared over their foreheads and were seen in varieties of turbans and baggy trousers. Some men appeared to look like women with their long skirts and hair. All in all, Singapore is a wide open town for the European high society.

Holy Indian bullocks, with humped backs and great horns, pulled the carts. Malay drivers broke segments of a bullock's tail to prevent the tail from knitting together and then they re-broke it until a double joint forms, thus preventing the bullock from flicking its tail without pain. The British government forbade breaking the bullocks' tail under punishment of the law, but Malays did it for the purpose of controlling the animals. They could pick up the tail and give it a twist to make the animal hurry up, or they could pick it up with a long, forked pole and do the same thing. It was painful for the bullock.

The Chinese outnumber all other nationalities in Singapore; they are the workers and the plutocrats. Their capital is invested in everything from canning pineapple to rubber-planting and ship-owning. The effluvia wafting to one's nostrils from the Chinese streets is essentially that of Canton City, or Soochow, mingled with odors of incense joss sticks, opium smoke, sandal wood, Chinese garbage, strange roots and vegetables, wood smoke, and the vapors from fried fish shops.

All these varied races had congregated here to toil under the equatorial sun. The straits-born Chinese were called *Babas*. Sikhs, who were night watchmen for stores and shops, were called *Djagas*, which means watchman. These men had no home other than the pavement in front of the store. During the day, their plain wooden cot leaned up against a pillar of the building while they lolled about, tended their pastured goats nearby, and conversed with fellow *Djagas*. When night came and the shop closed, they placed their beds against the doorway. They cooked their suppers over a little charcoal or wood fire on the sidewalks, and then pulled a light cover over themselves and went to sleep - right on the sidewalk outside. So, at night, the streets were filled with sleeping watchmen on little cots. The *Djagas* had their own goats grazing in adjoining patches. Just this supplied them with almost everything they needed.

The drive to Government Hill, or the Gap, past native sections of fine vegetation and hills was lovely. There was a splendid view of the harbor. A stop at the Botanical Gardens showed us exquisite trees and plants, fan-shaped Traveler's Palm, bamboo and coconuts. Small monkeys jumped in trees and came to the lawn to be fed. Cavanagh Bridge, over Singapore River, had no end of native boats and sampans under it.

Tamils were the dockhands, unloading and loading vessels. They were a colorful, motley and fearful-looking crowd with wild, long black hair, black bodies, red caste marks, and printed calico skirt sarongs wound around their legs. The first impressions as the boat docks were vividly colorful.

Style of Foreign Houses in Singapore

Our hosts, Mr. and Mrs. Ginsberg had a house built on a slope of a hill with extensive gardens filled with hedges, bamboo, palms, coconuts and mangos. There was an air of openness to the rooms, with open windows and doors, high ceilings, and matted floors, and a huge verandah all around. There were tile floors in the bathrooms with a huge glazed crock filled with clear water under a water tap with a dipper to throw water over oneself. Large mosquito netting hung over all the beds. People lived more on verandahs than indoors. Everything was open so the wind could blow through the entire house

Mr. and Mrs. Aaron's house, on the seashore, was surrounded by acres of coconut and rubber trees. The workers were Malay natives who lived in huts in the groves. Rubber was processed by tapping rubber trees, and then the raw or crude rubber was hung out on lines to dry. The raw rubber looked like mats and smelled strongly. The house resembled old Spanish or Italian architecture with whitewashed beams and ceilings and tile floors. These all opened to a view of the sea. Small, native craft and ships could be seen from the balcony. The huts of native servants were located behind the house.

Our New Years Eve was spent in Singapore where we went to a local *Coney Island* type of establishment called, "The New World." There we found sideshows, chance games run by Chinese, Chinese theaters, restaurants out in the open, dancing floors or cabarets, modern jazz vaudeville, acrobatics and native Malay plays. We enjoyed the plays best of all. The plays were accompanied by a weird musical accompaniment of drums, deep-sounding gongs, cymbals and wooden sticks. The acting with masks was much like children playing - in their speaking and singing, and then reciting in a chant and all the while moving the hands in the most exquisitely, graceful movements. They had the most expressive hands I have ever seen.

*****

Singapore to Mentok, Banka

It took Joe several days of hard work to secure deck passage on the K. P. M. Plancius to Mentok. The ticket officials at the Singapore K. P. M. office thought him rather crazy for asking for such a thing. Joe worked a bluff saying he wanted actual experience to write about, so they gave the three men deck-class, but refused it to Tonia. She had to go second class.

Here in the Far East, the steamship companies saw to it that white people (we assume Europeans) travel only first- or second-class. Third class or deck is "reserved" for the natives. After a few days of hard running around and a good deal of persuasion, we cajoled the K.P.M., or the Dutch Mail Line officials, into giving us deck passage from Singapore to the Island of Banka on the spic and span S.S. Plancius, which was as white and shining as a Dutch kitchen. We didn't show ourselves in the K.P.M. office any more for fear the agent would have a change of heart and make us buy second-class tickets. We sent our baggage on ahead to wait for us in Panang for an indefinite time, because we expected many months to go by before we reached that city. A knapsack each is all we carried. We had made plans for extensive hiking in the Indies, especially on the Island of Bali, so we traveled lightly.

The crush of the crowd getting on the launch was terrific, and the surf was rough as well. It was too rough on the one side of the Plancius to board and the gangplank was being continuously crushed by the bouncing launch. We finally got aboard after about a half hour. Before boarding Plancius, Tonia became sea sick and there was an order from the officers on the gangplank to "make way for the lady." An abrupt, snappy officer took our passports, but since Joe and I had but one passport between us, it confused the officer because Joe's ticket was deck and my ticket was second class. The officers' manners were gruff to us and as stiff as their high, white duck collars. They treated the native passengers like cattle with loud, rough shouts. It hurt us to see this boorishness because these natives were tidy-looking, orderly and quiet. We stood in the first-class foyer while all the "respectable" passengers disappeared into their cabins. The officers didn't know exactly what to do with us since we were the first whites to have gone deck on their boat. Here we encountered, for the first time, the meaning of that formidable phrase, "white prestige," in the Far East. A white man was supposed to uphold that prestige no matter from where he hailed. If he didn't, he was either forced through pressure (that is snubbed and avoided) or sent back from whence he came.

At last, a deck-officer pointed the way to our quarters and left us to our own resources to find some place midst the already-full deck space at the stern of the boat. It was certainly a most picturesque sight there. Instead of a deck floor, we saw an array of color — the blues and tans of sarongs, the brown of faces and limbs, and bright fiber baskets. People were stretched out everywhere. These Malays had spread their mats and thin blankets already, and what space they didn't use was taken up by their bundles, sacks, and eatables. We picked our way over this crowd of people, and no sooner did we stop at the far end of the deck than the natives jumped up and readily made room for us. They were clean, neat, and not a bad lot of neighborly fellow passengers to be squeezed in with at all.

The ship's officers were in a peculiar predicament. They did not want to see whites "degraded" before the natives, so they brought us a rough table and a bench to raise our status "above" that of the Malays. It was a great condescension, indeed, for that is never done for deck passengers. They even spoke a little with us. That table and bench wasn't brought up to us out of any kindness or out of any concern for our comfort. Instead, it was to "save face," as they say in China. When night came, we were brought a tin plate of rice and a few hunks of meat. Coffee arrived in one jagged-edged tin-can that was to do for both of us. This was another favor on the part of the ship's officers because the natives had to go below to fetch food in their own containers. It was the kindness of the Malays in offering us their own fruits and sweets that showed in contrast, the harsh, uncivil reception given us by the K. P. M. officers. With our few words of Malay, we conversed with the natives. Most of them were returning to their homes in Java. The tin mines and rubber plantations north of Singapore were shut down, and there was no more work for them.

All the children were washed in buckets before going to bed. The older folk changed into fresh sarongs and hung up their used ones to air for the night. It was remarkable how orderly and immaculate they all were in spite of the lack of any sanitary arrangements for them. There was a special section provided for the Chinese deck passengers on a lower level and in the hold of the ship. They made their quarters filthy and smelly in no time.

(Tonia wrote) My cabin was spacious but just barely clean and devoid of bunk curtains. It was a depressing and dismal place. A neat little Javanese steward, dressed in white duck trousers and coat with a batik tied around the waist and a batik square made into a perky cap, brought me tea and cakes. I felt miserable, first from the seasickness on the launch, and then because the guys had such a rotten place. The weather was stormy, and I felt so lonely in my cabin. All the guys' baggage, hats, and cameras were stored in my cabin. I went to look for Joe, but couldn't find him. I was appalled at the crowded decks.

(Joe wrote) When we got on board, we found the boat already filled with natives who had, no doubt, embarked at some previous port. They were stretched out on cots on the upper deck as well as on the one below. A talkative Chinese steward showed us the first-class cabins. The boat had only two or three and they were so stuffy and smelled so of varnish that we couldn't breathe. From the looks of these musty cabins and judging from the way the doors were stuck fast, it seemed that they had never been occupied. The few second-class cabins already were engaged by some Chinese merchants. So, we decided to make ourselves comfortable on the deck space next to the locked up dining salon belonging to first-class. This was railed off and had the luxury of a table and a few chairs. We found a stack of folded cots and took two of them for the night. The weather was beautiful, and we knew we would fully enjoy the night on deck. Let the cabins remain locked for all we cared. In this climate a cabin is a plagued nuisance anyway.

The steward then brought us pink tickets printed in Chinese and asked us for two florins per person. Imagine, going to Sumatra on an overnight passage for about eighty cents! Somehow taking deck passage again elated us. We felt like happy buccaneers who owned the boat. No food was furnished to deck passengers, but the little Chinese steward assured us he could bring us "*vely fine suppel.*" The tray he brought up was laden with savory food, and we felt like kings dining as we did with the open sea around us.

The wind blew fiercely at us in spite of the canvas covering the sides of the deck. All night long these Malays sang and played sweet, melancholy music. We dozed and slept, now and then waking up to turn over to a more comfortable position. There was nothing soft about that deck.

Every half hour during the night, an officer paced back and forth near us. They were not able to figure us out as yet. Perhaps, they feared we were up to some mischief amongst the natives. Still, the interesting experience was worth the discomfort and so was the enormous difference in fare. The K. P .M. Line had a monopoly in these waters and charged exorbitant prices. Deck was less than one fourth the cost of second-class fare.

(Tonia wrote) First-class was definitely divided from second-class though on the same deck. There was a rather rigid attitude. The second-class on this boat, with its regulations and divisions, gave the feeling that it was inferior, and only inferior people traveled so. There was nothing gracious or friendly as we experienced on other liners. I went on deck and found the guys. The officers gave them a separate place on deck, or rather tried to find one. But they gave up seemingly confused as to what to do. They brought two benches, a table, tin plates, and a mountain of rice with hunks of meat. Joe ate only rice. Tea was brought in an ordinary tin oil can with only one tin cup. There was no friendliness from the officers on the K. P. M. boat. On other boats, this situation would have been different and the boys would have been made comfortable and questioned about their interesting experiment. The boys slept as best they could, as they had no under bedding and not enough blankets. All night, officers passed by to see if they were still in their place, or perhaps fearing they were up to some mischief.

The supper bell rang. I was called down one deck to the dining room which was not very crowded. There was only one long table, half occupied with uninteresting people, half-castes mainly, some Persian merchants and Americans. The meal was graced with small talk. A very good Dutch meal was served. The dining room was cramped, so I went on deck to see the boys. They were located near a canvas partition that separated the classes. I went to sleep worrying about Joe. There was a storm during the night.

The next morning, the guys came in, one by one, to my second-class bathroom to shave and dress. Very early that morning the steward brought coffee to the cabin. After I dressed, I went on deck to the writing room but was asked to go to the second-class writing room as this was first-class. There, I found a Persian-Muslim busy swaying and reciting his prayers, but I sat down beside him and did my writing. Afterwards I went back to the stateroom, and hurriedly packed. The guys came, got their equipment, and then we all went to the foyer. There we got our passports back just in time.

A small launch pulled alongside the S. S. Plancius, and several Dutch island officials came aboard along with a handful of passengers who were going to Java. We saw some "real" Dutch people come aboard—children, grown ups, and servants. As we waited to get our passports back, we could overhear the ship's officers tell the land officials, in Dutch, about the peculiar white passengers. Finally, after half an hour on pins and needles, we heaved a sigh of relief and we were permitted to leave the Plancius. We stepped down the steep side-plank into the launch which took us, the only passengers to be seen, to Mentok. It was a mutual good riddance. We were glad to leave the Plancius. Her officers were all the more pleased to see the last of us.

Mentok

January 7, 1932

(Joe wrote) From Singapore we, during our sleep, had sailed in and out among the numerous isles of the Malay Archipelago, and dropped anchor very early the next morning in sight of Mentok[1] on the island of Banka. It was a typical South Sea island vista as seen from our boat - a palm-fringed beach curved around the pale-colored still water, and tall coconut palms. The sun was hot and the air thick with tropical moisture. There were a few little bungalows on plots of ground half-cleared of jungle growth. Since we had been told to go directly to the immigration offices, we disembarked carrying our own baggage and found the customhouse near the landing place. We carried our knapsacks to a moldy, worm-eaten little custom shed and left them in the care of a sad-faced Javanese in the Dutch service.

Well, we never realized what a time of it we were going to have when we went inside the immigration offices. The officers were supercilious and suspicious, most likely because the boys had chosen deck class. But, we had to face the taciturn Dutchman. He took our passports and began a cross examination that lasted all morning. The formalities of our entering the Dutch East Indies were rendered even more difficult for us because we traveled "deck." He didn't want to admit us to the Dutch colonies even though we already had a visa and had given the necessary security of 250 Dutch guilders per person in Singapore. When we showed him a substantial letter of credit, he was surprised and still more puzzled why we came "deck-class." He was sure that there was something "rotten in Denmark,"

You can imagine how our hearts sank when he told us that he couldn't, on his own authority, give us an answer there and then whether we could go on to Sumatra as we had planned. "You will have to wait on the island a few days anyway before the next boat comes in, so you may as well make yourselves comfortable and see the sights. Just before leaving, he ordered us to bring two passport photos of exact dimensions for his files. As we didn't have any extra ones with us, we asked him if there was a photographer in Mentok. As he carefully locked our passports in his drawer, he answered disinterestedly, "No, I don't think so. *Tot weerziens*, good day."

We left our baggage at the customs' house and took a walk in Muntok. It was damp, hot and steamy. The official had told us of the *pasangrahan*[2] to stop in, and also, that there was one Chinese hotel that we could tolerate. It was midday, and the town was asleep. Only one khaki uniformed Malay policeman was about barefoot and wearing a big straw hat turned up jauntily on one side.

As we looked for the hotel, an Indian boy came and spoke to us in English. He took us upstairs to see the rooms in the Chinese hotel. What a horrible place — rotten, bare wooden floor with thin wood partitions, and lousy beds with filthy mattresses. No other furniture! We left in disgust!

In the sultry heat, we walked about one mile to the *pasangrahan*. Joe made use of his Dutch and came to terms with the Dutch woman manageress for rooms and one meal a day. We got good drinking water and refreshed ourselves. There were huge beds in the room. We spent the rest of the afternoon resting, writing, and washing up. This was some contrast to the filthy Chinese inns!

We tried to come to terms with a Chinese photographer. Several people were called in to interpret, but we had no luck! We went away not ordering any photos - even though we had to have them.

In a furious state of mind we went back to fetch our knapsacks in that rickety customs house and had our ire pricked still more because our bags were turned upside down, inside out, and everything in them minutely examined, even the tooth brushes and sponges. What a mess! If we had come with labeled suitcases, we would have been kow-towed to, but knapsacks - bah!

We then went to the *pasar*[3] to buy fruit. There we saw small rickety shacks sheltered mountains of bananas and tropical fruit, jack fruit, durian, etc. Kitchen stalls were dirty, messy, and nobody spoke Dutch. We bought bananas and pineapples, took a taxi from the *pasar* to the customhouse, and then came back to the *pasangrahan*. We all washed up and ate our lunch of fruit. We ordered our evening meal that night, but the boys were most disappointed at the small amount served. We devoured everything on the table and asked for more and more bread.

We had seen how foreigners try to keep cool in the tropical heat of Singapore, but here in Muntok we got our first experience of the Dutch modes of living in the tropics. The *pasangrahan* is run by Hollanders, and they gave us comfortable accommodations. Each room had its own veranda with special reclining cane chairs, an awning, a tile floor and ventilators near the ceiling to make the air in the room bearable. Everything was clean as a pin especially the great double bed draped with mammoth mosquito netting. There were long, hard bolster pillows which everybody here placed under their knees at night to keep a bit more air circulating under the body while sleeping. These were called, humorously enough, "dutchmen." Solemn-faced Javanese were the servants here waiting upon us at the table and cleaning the rooms.

For nearly all their food supplies, the *pasangrahan* and the few Dutch families were dependent upon the bi-weekly K.P.M. shipments. Fresh meats, canned goods, hams, preserves, and butter, all came from Holland; they had a tiny ice plant near the custom shed that kept their precious supplies fresh a little bit longer. That colony of foreigners was literally dependent upon the liners for most of their needs.

What a monotonous life for a handful of foreigners! On this island there were twenty-five pure Dutch and about thirty-five mixed, or Eurasians. One of the officials of the big tin mining company of Banka lived in the room next to ours. He came back from the mines early in the afternoon each day, got into cool cotton pajamas, and sat on his porch playing, over and over again, the same operatic arias on a little portable phonograph. He told us that tin is the main product of this island and that the mines are owned and operated by the Dutch government. Before the slump, they netted a clear profit of twenty-seven million guilders, or around eleven million dollars per year.

His two sons were going to school in Java while his wife lived in Holland. His life was much the same as that of countless others in the colonial service — families forced to be separated while life ran on monotonously and uneventfully. His first ten years in the colonies as an army officer were more interesting because he had made so many expeditions to inaccessible places and islands. But life had become "pretty dull" now. He was anxiously waiting for his son to grow up and take over his commission. As soon as that happened, he would be returning to Europe immediately. Thank God!

The only amusements for the Hollanders here were small parties, card games, or the phonograph. Their loneliness was pathetic. There was nothing to do but live from day to day with no change of sights, people or new conversational topics. They were even deprived of the usual influx of visitors, for hardly any tourists touched this isle. Many of them would have gladly spoken to us if Joe hadn't been wearing khaki shorts. And of course, the story of our knapsacks and deck passage had been whispered about so we were avoided like the plague.

There was a party on the first night we were in the *pasangrahan*, and we were most carefully snubbed. On our veranda, we chuckled to ourselves as we listened to them sing all the Dutch folk songs they possibly could remember. They looked like wooden people as they danced rigidly and clumsily trying to make merry. You know these large, overweight Dutchmen were not any too graceful. Why they insisted upon dressing up in stiff, uncomfortable duck suits in this hot climate, was more than we could see. Even for work in the mines, they didn't allow themselves any comfortable clothes as the English did in their colonies. There wasn't a Dutchman to be seen wearing shorts.

Banka was a most dreamy, steamy little island full of unruly jungle and wild animals. Flowers and tropical trees grew like weeds here—bananas, pineapple, and all sorts of unusual, tropical fruits. The little town of Mentok itself had few streets, but had a dirty little *pasar* with many kitchen stalls, frying bananas and bits of meat.

There was a large Chinese population in Mentok partly due to the mines. One day we noticed a sign reading: "Chinese Official Headquarters." Upon inquiry we found that the Chinese are given a great deal of responsibility in governing themselves since there were so many Chinese on the island. One of them was selected as the headsman and given authority to hear all of his peoples' grievances and wants. He was, in turn, responsible to the Dutch government for their proper behavior and order as well as for the collection of taxes and other levies that went to the government. This was a Dutch policy that was carried out in all of their colonial possessions and made for a more harmonious rule where there were different cultural elements to be governed.

Here in Mentok the tangled vegetation grew down to the sea amid warm swamps. Fish nets lay spread out to dry on the smelly beach, or hung from poles behind the dwellings. The natives were fairly clean, but their pure Malay stock had long been mixed with that of the Chinese and aborigines so that these Bankanese were now not as beautiful. We noticed a few small, kinky-haired natives, called *Orang Sekah.* They told us that they were the original Sumatran aborigines who inhabited this island before the Malay came. The few still here lived in their handmade canoes and did nothing but fish. They had very dark skin and looked quite different from the Malay.

It was here that we saw our first Dutch colonial bungalows. They were, indeed, made for comfort in the tropics with thick stucco walls painted white and red tile roofs and verandas. The kitchen in the rear, was connected to the house by a cement or gravel walk covered over with a tiled roof supported on pillars. The Hollanders didn't mind the long walk between the kitchen and the dining room because they had many servants to attend to everything. The bath and toilet were usually on either side of the kitchen. What a luxurious feeling these baths gave us! We could splash and throw about all the water we wanted as we stood on a wooden lattice frame and dipped buckets full from the big cement tank. Four times a day was not too often for such a cool bath in this climate. One could walk all around the outside of the house and out to the bath and be protected from the frequent rains by the broad eaves of the tile roofs.

Next morning, as we went to the market to buy fruit, we walked through the town. There was an abundance of foliage, very neat huts, and colorful gardens. We bought our fruit as it began to drizzle, and walked back to the *pasangrahan*. Everything steamed!

Tonia discovered she had left her sweater in the photographer's shop, so we went back and found it on the same chair in the shop. The guys went back to town to get the baggage we had left at the customhouse.

In the morning of the third day, we walked to the K. P. M. office to find out about a Chinese boat going to Sumatra. A brusque, but obliging official asked us if we needed any help. Once more, before the authority of the immigration, we had to fill out long papers that had such questions as, "where was your grandmother born?" After new cross-examinations, the official forgot his self-importance for a minute and became a human and smiled. He thought us adventurous, but nevertheless, harmless rascals, and gave us the official permit which would carry us through the Dutch East Indies. We felt as if we had just won a feather in our cap.

The official couldn't understand why we needed additional photos, so he phoned the immigration official. He verified it and said he didn't know of the "new law." He sent his servant to call the Chinese photographer. When we told him what difficulties we had, the servant came and helped us explain what we needed. The Chinese boat left that afternoon at 4 o'clock and the photographer had promised the photos at 2 o'clock so, we hurried to his dumpy shop.

We had to get our photos to the immigration official, and by frantic hand language and sputtering Malay, we finally had in our hands the most woebegone pictures of ourselves we had ever seen. We went back to his shop, and since he was the only photographer in town, we decided to have extra photos made. We had a lot of fun posing for photos. A small schoolgirl (Chinese & Malay) helped us speak to the photographer to settle terms.

We went back to *pasangrahan*, took lunch, packed, and returned to the photographers in a taxi. The photos were done, so we drove to the immigration office to have our entrance paper fixed at last. The official became a bit more human and smiled. All was in order. We had our receipt for 250 gilders, entrance money, and all necessary papers.

We took several photos at the seashore where two small Malay boys proudly posed for us. Then we waited an hour by the pier for the "Sinang" to appear; but it was several hours before the boat was to come, so we took a long walk along the shore. Mentok was like the genuine South Sea tropical isle one reads about in novels— sleepy, lazy, dreamy palms, luxuriant tropical colors, and vegetation. The loneliness of the spot for European officials, however, was terrible for there was nothing to do but live from day to day with no change of conversation, sights, or new people. Hardly any tourists ever touched the isle.

A Chinese boat ran regularly between here and Palembang, Sumatra, but nobody could tell us anymore about it other than, "It's due here tomorrow." It will announce its arrival by tooting its whistle, and tickets would be sold only on board ship. The K. P. M. boats plied between all these islands, of course, but we were out for all kinds of experiences. So why not sail on a Chinese boat? We didn't care what these stiff and proper Dutchmen think of us, especially now that we had our entrance permit in our pocket. So, "sail Ho" for Sumatra.

We had almost given up on the Chinese boat, but finally arrived in Mentok. We had grown so weary of waiting for it together with many native passengers that we decided to take a stroll along the jungle shoreline. When we were a good distance away, we heard three blasts of the boat's whistle. We ran back, stumbling over coconuts and rotting wood, to catch the ship's launch, but it was already full of passengers and just chugging away as we reached the pier.

There were many natives still waiting, and all of them, like us, were trying to get into some sort of boat. After a few minutes of hurried bargaining, we found ourselves in a small dory packed with Malays and rowed by the same boy who had sold us bananas in the *pasar.* And so we boarded the launch. The boy was tickled about our seeing him in the "boat business" also. Everybody laughed and joked.

Since we had shipped our suitcases on to Penang by a "B&O" boat, we had only a small knapsack apiece. Kane had a real knapsack while we had the larger half of an army pup tent belonging to Lee. Lee had the other half. Alongside the rusty S.S. Senang, big nets hoisted our knapsacks with hundreds of other bundles and rolls of bedding, while we climbed up the gangplank. This Chinese boat had a Dutchman for its captain and first officer, but the rest of the crew were all Chinese.

We climbed up to the boat without tickets as we were to buy them on board. The boys went to look over the accommodations on board and found that the Malays had already taken nearly all the deck space. The top deck was full of cots, on which Malays made their quarters. The next deck below was just full and no cots. We took over just one part of the deck where there were chairs and a table. Kane found a cot and set it up, and we all decided to remain on deck as it was beautiful weather since the boat didn't leave until six o'clock. The Dutch officers didn't even say Boo! After a few hours, a little Chinese steward brought us pink tickets written in Chinese asking for two florins. We felt mighty smart getting overnight passage for what amounted to 80 cents gold. We found three more cots and set them up, pulled some deck canvas down. We were comfortable with our four cots placed with heads against the empty dining salon and our feet toward the railing. We asked the steward for chow when he had brought coffee. Deck passengers couldn't order food, but, he brought the boys a full, first-class meal for one gilder and for Joe and me, rice, eggs, and two bananas for one half gilder. It was marvelous on deck with the tropical breeze. We were in our own corner, and it felt like our own private yacht.

A Chinese boy came to clear off dishes and asked ten gilders for the meal and all four cots. We wouldn't listen but paid him for the meal only. He insisted, but gradually came down to six, and then, to two gilders apiece, but we all held firm threatening to go to the captain. The boy seemed afraid and actually embarrassed. He refused the tip we gave him for the meal. He went away, but came back later saying he wanted his cots. Kane's and Lee's cots were his. We told him to go ahead and take them which he did but he left ours saying, "You lady all right. If not have got money can have cot." So, the boys were left with no cots, but they later went out and brought two more. We took out our sweaters and blankets, and made ourselves comfortable for the night. It was so beautiful, though, we couldn't sleep.

The very fact that we took deck passage again elated us, especially Tonia, as she felt like a regular buccaneer. We felt as if we owned the boat, having a whole section of deck to ourselves, with table, chairs and cots. Not one word did the Dutch officers speak to us. We took flashlights, found the first-class bathroom and toilets, and washed ourselves for the night. A certain bravado and assuredness pervaded upon us, which seemed to become a part of our traveling characteristics from then on. That one night passage was unforgettable; first, for the freedom and joy felt in the deck passage, and secondly, for the mysterious beauty of that night as we steamed slowly up into the jungle-land of Sumatra.

Sumatra

January 12, 1932

It took about two hours for us to cross the channel and to the mouth of the Musi River of Sumatra. There was a clear sky as the boat entered the estuary. We were aware of the new, strange constellations. The Big Dipper was upside down. No Milky Way was visible. The Southern Cross shown overhead like a huge diamond, and all these stars were reflected, remarkably, in the water of the river. It was a fantastic and uncanny sight. The stars gave enough light to see the riverbank and small masses of vegetation which was carried down by the river. We could hardly believe we were going further and further into the wilds of Sumatra. Now and then lights, which bordered the riverbanks, made us wonder what they were. We arrived at Palembang just after sunrise.

Dawn gradually made the surroundings visible as we neared Palembang. The river was dotted with craft, and here and there we clearly saw palm-thatched huts huddled together perched high on stilts at the river's edge. Sometimes we could see an acre or two of cleared ground behind them; but for the most part, there was nothing but swampy jungle growing right up to their threshold. Soon we reached Palembang. The river was a beehive of traffic. We discovered that all trade and intercourse here was carried on by watercraft. The native Sumatrans live over and on the water.

Small canoes skimmed over the water, looking as frail as peanut shells. There was a sudden beehive of native water traffic and colorful activity spread out before our eyes. The muddy banks supported Sumatran huts in great number. We reached Palembang just after sunrise. That overnight trip, as we slowly steamed up the great

Musi River into the jungle-lands of Sumatra, will always remain an unforgettable trip for us - a night impregnated with phantom-like illusions of mysterious tropical beauty.

The sunrise arrival at Palembang was not without incident. Immigration officials came onboard. They were surprised to see us with packs. One boat officer told an official (in Dutch), "They went deck class." The immigration official asked who the bearded fellow was. They still couldn't figure us out. There were no customs formalities there.

Palembang was a unique place - a city floating on the water of the Musi River and built over it - like a primitive, tropical Venice, heated by a broiling sun and cooled by torrents of rains. This Musi is a tremendous river. Big boats could navigate its winding, snake-like, course for miles, but they had to heed the river's tides, its strong currents, and treacherous sand bars. The vastness of this body of water inspired us with overpowering awe. The river wound like a sluggish monster. The swampy jungle was flat, and there were no hills or mountains to break up the endless monotony of this landscape. We saw almost nothing but sky and brown water, with only a green strip of jungle-covered land at the horizon.

One part of the city was built on dry ground. There we found the usual Chinese-owned stores and all sorts of merchandise and wares in Dutch, tropical style bungalows, and *kantoors* or "Dutch offices." There were oil refineries, coal yards, and the beginning of the railway going to all parts of Sumatra. But all this human enterprise and mechanical activity was simply lost in insignificance beside the immensity of this jungle and its river. If the native canoes seemed like peanut shells, then the big steamers looked no larger than shoe boxes afloat.

The most interesting part of Palembang was the native section. And we could not see it by walking in the streets for there were no "streets," as we used the term. Palembang's lanes and avenues were the water canals, and the Musi was the highway. The houses were built over the water, either on bamboo foundations that are fastened to piles or high over the river on stilts. The waterway between two rows of dwellings was a street. These streets didn't extend back from the main river very far, (perhaps a dozen huts deep) for the jungle, even at Palembang, grew thick at its edge.

What a thrill it was to skim over this swift river in a clean-cut, shallow canoe paddled by a short, strong-limbed Sumatran. Every boatman seemed to sit in the water, as he balanced on a thin, tail-like projection at the stern while propelling his craft with a short-handled triangular paddle. The activity, carried on all day long on the Musi River, tributaries and canals, was astonishing. The trading and bartering center hummed as it attracted not only the citizens of Palembang, but also Sumatrans for miles around. If the natives wanted to shop, they paddled along "Main Street" to the row of floating Chinese stores. The shops were attractively displayed, just like any in ordinary shops. But there on the river, customers had to bargain either from their boats, or else tie up to a post and step onto a floating store.

There wasn't one morning that didn't find us at Palembang's floating *pasar*. Frail dugouts and large *sampans*⁴ loaded with fruits, vegetables, chickens, tobacco, and fiery red peppers, with yams. Crabs, fish, and shrimp came in large numbers each morning from far and near. Fishermen didn't unload and sell on the land but gathered at the same spot near the river bank for their daily marketing. In the first place, there wasn't dry land to unload onto. Then because their customers came by canoe, the market was conducted on the water. It was a vivid and colorful sight.

Sampans had grass roofs ending at a point like a duck's tail. Some of these small craft were used as permanent dwellings by families. There were big and little house-boats with women watching their cook pots and tending their children. All of these differently-shaped boats, which lined the banks, housed much of Palembang's population. When the market canoes crowded in around these boats, it was a riot of color with brilliant Sumatran head-dresses, women's shawls, colorful fruits, live fish, and little scarlet peppers in huge piles on the sampans. The buyers, in their paper-shell canoes, paddled from one vendor to the other. A woman picked up a live fish from the bottom of her skiff which was half filled with water. Crafts moved in and out continually, and the chatter and bargaining was lively. These Sumatrans used their water crafts expertly, maneuvering, turning and backing them up on the crowded river without so much as a bump. This was one of the most interesting market scenes we had ever seen.

The natives, having finished the marketing, paddled home with purchases tied in neat packages using old newspapers that came, strangely enough, from England and America. The women's purchases were neatly placed on the flat floor boards of the canoe. It seemed they never failed to bring home a little pile of scarlet chili-peppers on a scrap of paper or banana leaf. Usually, their large straw hat was placed over their purchases protecting them from the sun or the hard and sudden rains that came so regularly. Their wants were few. The important thing to them was to have a river-worthy and attractive-looking craft.

Many tradesmen, like carpenters and tinsmiths, plied their trade from sampans that held their workshops and tools. It was a beautiful sight to see a large boat carrying five or six people bound for who knows where. The women held umbrellas over their heads, and were probably dressed in their best.

These sampans had shallow sides, and they looked like graceful splinters skimming across the water when seen from the shore. The river craft plied back and forth all day long. Going upstream was difficult, but so was going directly across the river in a straight line. We continued to admire the skill with which these natives managed to cross the swift current. They paddled obliquely, cleverly aiming much further upstream beyond the point of their destination. They judged, quite accurately, the force of the mighty river.

There were also many two-storied river boats, propelled by large water wheels. They looked comical as they plied the river, blissfully disregarding currents or difficulties. The passengers seemed to enjoy these rides and sang and shouted, having regular festive parties on their trips. The only other motor-driven craft on the Musi (beside the passenger liners) were a few swift launches belonging to Dutch companies and the government. The K. P. M. Line had a few small steamers that plied the upper reaches of the Musi. They ran mainly conducting government inspection work, but they had a few accommodations for passengers as well.

Palembang, like Mentok, had many Chinese residents. These Chinese were, for the most part, rich merchants. The rest of them seemed to be coolies who were used mainly for hard labor. It was remarkable how clannish and patriotic these Chinese were in spite of the fact that they had been away from China for generations. Just two days ago, all their stores were decorated with Chinese and Dutch flags, and they chartered all the waterwheel boats of Palembang. These were loaded to capacity going up and down the Musi with banners flying and bands playing. All this was to celebrate a Chinese victory over the Japanese in Shanghai. Some of these white-jacketed Chinese shopkeepers were much wealthier than they looked. Many of them sent their boys to Java and even to China to study. A remarkable people these Chinese.

The Sumatrans are Mohammedans and their house of worship is called a *missegit*. Palembang's *missegit* was situated on the high dry, part of the river's bank, but it extended over the water just the same. There was a little pier extending from the building, as the *missegit's* main entrance was from the river. Nearly all the worshippers came by canoe. On Friday, their day of rest, we could see a continuous stream of people going up and down this pier. The canoes were tied to the pier in rows that were three and four deep. Small fishing villages along the Musi had their own *missegits.* They were smaller, of course, and were set up on piles high above the water, just like their huts. Although they were palm-thatched, the roofs of the these village *missegits* are of the same design as that of the large one in Palembang, which had a sloping square, double-tiered roof of corrugated iron.

Early, one bright morning, we decided it was time to leave Palembang and see more of Sumatra. We had a hurried rush, by taxi, through the city to catch the ferry. A small ferry launch went upstream to the point where the railway began. On this ferry ride, our eyes lingered for the last time on the picturesque river life on the Musi as seen in the cool morning freshness before the sun began to beat down.

As we arrived on time, Joe ran to get the tickets to take us to Oosthaven and Merak[5] in Java. The ferry waited for us for several minutes while Joe got the tickets. Finally he appeared, and we all got on the ferry. When the ferry began to move away from the pier, Joe suddenly said, "I have to go back." Wherewith, he jumped from the railing of the ferry onto the pier. The ferry kept on going, and Joe had the tickets. We would miss the train! Kane, frantically gestured to the ferry pilot, and the ferry actually turned back. We saw Joe standing at the landing awaiting the ferry. He jumped back on board once more, and we were finally off. I demanded an explanation! He had made that crazy maneuver because he had been short-changed ten guilders and felt he had to go back to get it. When the agent saw him come back, he came to meet Joe on the landing with the change. There was about four anxious minutes for all of us.

When we landed, the train was ready to start. Sumatran trains had only first-class (*witte kaartjees*) or white tickets and second-class native fares *(inlander kaartjes)* or green tickets. There was no third-class for foreigners. An islander could purchase a white ticket by paying the small difference, but the accommodations were practically the same. Having separate divisions kept up the white-colonial prestige. The train was very clean and comfortable. Native stewards dressed in white jackets and trousers, a batik cap, a sash around the waist, and barefooted like those onboard K. P. M. Line.

A stream of vendors walked up and down outside the train with baskets of food. We bought two ripe pineapples for our breakfast just as the train slowly pulled out. We ordered breakfast and, along the way at a stop, bought five more sweet pineapples for f.10. from the vendors who came to the train windows.

We traveled through miles and miles of jungle. From the window, there was nothing to see but miles of vines and parasitic creepers forming a solid green canopy draped from tree-top to tree-top. Now and then, a tiny station and clusters of huts broke the monotony. Finally we arrived at Prabumulih where we took a break in our journey until four in the afternoon. We set out to explore this tiny Sumatran village.

This station was too small for a check room so we left our baggage with the stationmaster and had all the Sumatran officials trying to do things for us. We bought stamps which caused confusion as to what stamps were needed for Singapore, America, or Hong Kong. They probably thought we were Dutchmen, but Joe with his Dutch and Malay phrase book managed to get along nicely.

We then began our exploration of our first small Sumatran village. When walking down one little street, the first thing we found was a small native jewelry shop. There were two men squatting on the floor creating ornaments of dipped gold and silver on brass, over a tiny flamed burner. We talked with them in our three words of Malay, and examined the few trinkets on display. They had good designs.

Then we walked further into the heart of the village. The streets were mere lanes winding between grass and bamboo huts. In the courtyard of one hut we saw many people picking strange fruit. We stopped to watch, and they came to offer some to us. The fruit was round and prickly like a chestnut, orange-red on the outside and on the inside; it was slippery and pale-green. It was delicious tasting — like lemon and banana. We were impressed with the simple native kindness to us strangers. They spoke to us and tried to help us understand them. Tonia had some Japanese bean candy, and she cut some into slices and offered it to them. They would not take it at first, but after she ate a piece and showed them that it was not harmful, they took some and relished it.

Women and children quietly gazed at us from open windows, or peeped out from their doorways. Some ventured out as far as the road, but when we tried to snap photos, they quickly disappeared. We explored the crooked lanes between the raised huts. The lanes followed curves between coconut palms. Their huts were four feet off the ground, standing on thick logs, as a protection against wild animals. A narrow ladder gave access to its one room. Often a beautifully carved balcony was built on one side of the house with the roof of palm thatch. These gentle natives gazed at our cameras with wonderment. A sudden shower came, and we sought shelter beneath what looked like a village community meeting place.

The *Kompong* was so clean. (*Kompong can mean either a cluster of huts or a village.*) There were a few water buffalo roaming about as well as dogs, cats, chickens, and tamed pet monkeys. There were no fences anywhere, and the animals freely browsed. There were no pigs to be seen as the people were Mohammedans. There wasn't a bad odor anywhere. We noticed the many tropical fruits such as jackfruit, durian, breadfruit, and hundreds of other varieties growing out of tree trunks.

Most of the huts had nicely-carved balconies and interiors as neat as a pin. They contained no furniture except for a few woven mats to sit and sleep on, nothing more. Wood was the fuel for cooking on an earthen hearth in one corner of the hut. The smoke escaped through the thatch and bamboo walls making that particular corner very black, of course. We saw a girl, shy as a deer, hulling rice by pounding a long log up and down in a hollow wooden or stone mortar.

The women wore brilliant cotton sarongs and thin jackets. The men, also, wore sarongs or sometimes wide trousers made from the same brilliant batik cotton. The Sumatrans wove and dyed cloth differently from that of the Javanese.

These Sumatrans were as curious as children, unspoiled and kind, probably never having seen many tourists before. The natives in Prabumulih, however, seemed naïve and shy. We chanced upon a large group of women dressed in brilliant colors. Their sarongs were draped high enough to cover their breasts, leaving their shoulders bare. A few wore thin-white jackets that were open in front. Great gold discs hung around their necks, and ornaments decorated their black hair. They, smilingly, showed us their cute 'roly-poly' babies, who were dressed in bead and coin necklaces, bangles, anklets, and a tiny metal mesh apron the size of a leaf, dangling in front from a string around their stomach. However most of them ran about naked until eight or ten years of age. The men and older boys, like the women, also wore sarongs or sometimes wide pantaloons made from brilliant cotton batik, which was a Javanese product.

We happened upon a little native one-room school house. We were greeted and treated as if we were important Dutch officials. We went inside and were saluted. The small boys craned their necks to see us, and the teacher blushed and was confused. The little boys were sitting on hard benches and were wearing black velvet Malay caps. The teacher was a young boy, who was all smiles but spoke no Dutch. Most of the teachers taught only in Malay language. There were drawings and watercolors around the room done by the students. They were exceptionally clever and artistic. The teacher had the children stand and salute us as we went out. They were excited over our visit; as *orange blands* (or white people) rarely stepped into their schoolroom.

There were only two places to purchase food at the village. We had decided not to take any food from the hotel keeper as his prices were too high. The native stands offered very little.

Two young boys showed us their water hole, or bath. It was a beautiful deep-green pool surrounded by thick vegetation. There was a log platform with a palm roof and log steps which lead to the water. A group of women and children went down to fill their black gourds. They poured water over their babies and lapped up water for drinking by throwing it into their mouths with three fingers. The boys filled some black hollow gourds and offered us some water. But we didn't drink. They were eager to show us everything but yet were reserved and distant. They posed proudly for their photos. We had been able to snap a photo of a small Chinese-Malay shop in one of the *Kompongs* with many naked babies crawling about.

The natives clearly looked happy, well fed, and satisfied. No one toiled. There was very little land cultivated. These natives were not spoiled by tourists or western influences. They moved freely with a grace of carriage. We fell in love with them. No one molested us or even followed us very much.

We saw wild monkeys for the first time here in Prabumulih.[6] We must have surprised a group of them on the ground near some huts. What a chattering and rushing came about as they leaped and swung by their tails, reaching the high branches of the jungle trees in a few seconds.

There was no Dutch *pasangrahan* in Prabumulih, only a tiny inn which was run by a Javanese. How proud he was of his two solitary guest rooms. All the furniture was enclosed inside a 'box-like' smaller room, made of screen wire that stood in the very middle. Each of these two big rooms had a screen door. He assured us we would never be bothered by mosquitoes once we were inside the enclosure. Although we felt like rats in a cage, we had to admit to the advantage of being able to sit at the table in comfort while all the hungry mosquitoes buzzed on the outside. Our innkeeper concocted meals from tinned foods that came from Australia and Holland. One day, we decided to find our lunch in the village pasar. But there really was no regular pasar with open booths and produce, so we went up to the only tiny store in the village run by a Chinese man and his Sumatran wife. His rough shelves had a few sarongs, sandals, rock salt, chili peppers, soap, pineapples, and a few candles. He found some boiled duck eggs for us, and with a few pineapples and a small sticky bun, we went over to a quiet field and ate our lunch on a log. Goats came up to share it with us.

Though grocers were few, this *kompong*[7] had a jewelry shop. There on the floor, two craftsmen sat on mats with a tiny flame between them. Over this flame they twisted and bent brass wire, devising earrings and bangles, and hammered away at other ornaments. Most of these objects were later plated with silver and gold. They proudly brought a little drawer filled with all the trinkets they had on hand. Most of them were of the same design we had seen the village women wearing. Their earrings, especially, were ingenious.

Everybody we saw looked well-fed and satisfied in Prabumulih. Nobody we saw worked hard and there didn't seem to be any Western exploitation to any marked degree. How different were these happy Sumatrans in comparison to their brothers in the Federated Malay States, who toiled so hard and yet remained so poverty stricken. This little kompong, of about 400 souls, it housed one lonely Dutch official whose main duty was to collect the taxes. There was a peaceful, dreamy atmosphere in Prabumulih that made us want to remain there for days beneath its coconut palms. We really fell in love with these naive, child-like people and their easy-going primitive way of living.

Back at the station, we waited for the train as we sat and wrote notes. We tried to get something to drink at a nearby stand, but the lemonade was vile-looking, so we drank some more vile-tasting soda water. At least it was bottled. The sun and heat were great and everything steamed. But even so, we were really sorry to leave this peaceful place, but we looked forward to seeing more Sumatran villages.

We boarded the train for Martapura. It was a pleasant ride through the lush jungle foliage with the view always the same, but never the same. There were sections with overhanging trees, then sections with the tall tiger grass, but always the green lush, hot-humid atmosphere.

All trains in the Dutch East Indies had a buffet car. The waiters brought a lengthy menu card, and we saw a page of first-class, second-class and third-class refreshments. There was:

First-Class Koppie (coffee) — Second-Class Koppie —Third-Class Koppie, (with abundant grounds in the bottom) Koppie met melk, — zonder melk, — zuiker extra (with sugar)

Waater — 5 cents—Ijs Waater — 10 cents (ice water)—Stroop — (ice water with pink sugar syrup).

Brood zonder Boter — Brood met Boter — Brood met Broter und Kas

Kane and Lee were heavy eaters and often ordered native dishes of curried rice and meats from the buffet, but we usually took just tea or koppie and bread and butter. A hot Dutch meal could be obtained on express trains, where it was always brought to our seats, since there was no dining car.

Martapura

It was about dark when our train drew up to a station where we gathered our belongings and got off. This was a much larger place - a town almost - called Martapura. We never could travel straight through on the regular train between one important station and the next. The little villages and towns along the way had such a lure for us that it took us days to cover a distance that would otherwise require only a few hours to traverse. Besides, there was so much more to be seen by staying in these seldom-frequented places and mingling with the natives. We didn't want to miss anything.

From the moment we got off the train, a sickening putrid odor enveloped us. We couldn't imagine what it was and could hardly stand it, but there was no escape. That vile odor followed us everywhere even into the funny little hostel in which we stayed.

Our room was in a big barn-like structure with a high roof. Inside were many rooms partitioned off by sheets of corrugated iron on all four sides to a height of ten feet. Above that extended several feet of fine mesh chicken wire, which was stretched across the top to form a ceiling. This made each room like a cage enclosure. The fairly clean bed, draped in musty mosquito netting, took up most of the space in our room. In the rear of the inn was a big concrete tank filled with water, which together with a tin dipper, served as the bath. Such a disagreeable odor wafted in from the adjoining toilet that we could never really linger and enjoy the cooling bath.

A steady stream of curious villagers came by and questioned the innkeeper about us. Where did we come from? Who were we? They tarried around on the outside veranda hoping to catch a glimpse of us. Meanwhile, we washed up and decided to go find something for our supper, preferring to get our Sumatran experiences first-hand in a native inn. However we found a Dutch place — just a slice of miniature Holland — where we would have gotten good food and nothing more.

It was night already, and many dim lights lit up the one "business street" lined with shops as big as match boxes. We saw many Chinese eating houses, all of which were completely open in the front with neither door nor wall. But these little, dumpy restaurants were so filthy, and we simply didn't have the courage to eat the food. We walked the entire length of the town and came back still hungry. Next, we investigated the provision shops. These were run by Chinese, also, and by one or two red-faced Arabs. They seemed to have been stocked up with nothing else but stinking dried fish and messy dates full of straw. Twice we made the rounds of all the stores and found nothing appetizing enough to be eaten. In desperation, we finally rummaged on shelves and in boxes of the biggest Chinese epicurean shop and triumphantly went back to our tin room with the spoils.

A smoky kerosene lamp lit our table as we spread out the feast. But oh, our anticipation was premature. The tin of sardines was so ancient that we were afraid to eat it, and the brilliant yellow soda water was luke warm. So we filled up with hard tack biscuits and bananas. In spite of the sorry meal, we did have a great deal of fun finding it. Except for that awful odor, we would have been perfectly content. That odor came in like waves. We thought, perhaps, it came from goat cheese because the natives kept so many goats, and then we decided it was too strong even for that. It smelled like a mixture of sour Mexican pulque, vinegar, and jasmine. We determined to investigate the source of this smell next morning. We blew out the lamp and crawled beneath the mosquito netting.

The inn was locked up for the night and we heard the clanking of cross bars and boards being fitted back into place. No sooner was the last lamp put out, when a bedlam of ungodly noises began. Our hairs stood on edge! Live creatures seemed to be racing about, scrambling above us and crawling up and down the iron walls. We sat up in bed striking matches, but we couldn't see a thing. A whole zoo seemed to have broken loose, banging and scratching against the corrugated iron. What was it, —monkeys—-rats—-tigers? We never found out that night, even though we burned up a whole box of matches. In the morning, our bananas, left from the night before, were all neatly scooped out with only their skins to remind us of them, and the hard tack biscuits had completely disappeared. We no longer made fun of the chicken wire over our heads after that. Think of the monkeys we would have had as companions in our room each night. For that's what they were: monkeys! (there were also huge rats, flying cockroaches, and snakes)

We went to the *pasar* in the morning with our noses leading the way to the source of that awful odor. There it was, piled up in great mounds all over the *pasar: durian fruit.* Natives came trotting in with loaded baskets, dumping more and more of the fruit on piles. These *durans* are greenish fruit about the size of an oblong, small watermelon. Their thick-prickly peeling and seeds lay about everywhere, and natives stood around relishing the white meat. They offered us some and we warily tasted it. If we held our noses, we might have enjoyed its flavor, which was strange but not disagreeable. However, we purchased fresh coconuts instead, split them open, and drank the milk. This is one of the most excellent thirst quenchers in the tropics. It was especially so when we had difficulties getting boiled water and it is dangerous for "whites" to drink any water in these latitudes.

A sturdy Sumatran showed us how he made his own cigarettes by rolling finely shredded tobacco into a long, thin straw-like stalk. It is remarkable with what simple things people can be content.

We got acquainted with the Sumatran stationmaster there. He was so overjoyed at white people taking the trouble to speak with him that he left the station in the hands of a subordinate for thirty minutes so that he could run home and bring us his photograph album to see. Although it didn't have many pictures, the few it did have meant much to him. This was a fine gesture on his part to show his friendliness toward us. After that, he invited us several times to sup with him at his house. We tried to be polite by bravely swallowing the fiery, highly-seasoned Sumatran dishes his wife prepared for us. We had him and his assistants jumping around one day because we had come to buy some stamps. They scratched their heads in a quandary as we had letters addressed to Hong Kong and the United States. They didn't know what stamps were necessary for those "unknown lands."

The main street of this village was lined with quite a few small Chinese shops and paved with asphalt. Everybody looked at us and gave us military greeting thinking we were all Dutch officials on an inspection tour. This happened all over Sumatra. A small *pasangrahan* was not far from the *pasar*, where a handful of officials lived—- (one *"pure"* Dutchman, and several Dutch-Javanese workers).

We saw a magnificent river in flood stage here in the village. It carried whole trees and undermined the high banks causing them to cave into the swirling water. We walked along the banks for a long way. Along the river's edge there was a long row of small, floating rafts and shelters that were moored to posts, and on these platforms the native women came to wash their laundry and themselves. They had to come down a steep embankment to reach the water. The Sumatrans bathed a great deal and were certainly very clean. The small shelters were used as water closets. Women also carried the river water back to their dwelling for cooking purposes and drinking. This water seldom became polluted because the river was always in a continuous flow, although it did get very brown with mud at times.

Every hut had its own canoe beside it, usually turned upside down on a raised platform when not in use. They were graceful crafts, hollowed out of big single logs. This little village was like all others in southern Sumatra, filled with magnificent tropical vegetation. The rains poured several times each day, but they never interrupted our hikes for long. Here also we saw pet monkeys, for some of the natives have as many as six chained in their yards.

We got acquainted with two Hollanders and some Eurasians who lived at the *pasangrahan*. Their attitude toward the Sumatrans was unexpected. They considered them good-for-nothings and lazy. And it was this Sumatran characteristic to take life easy and lull about that so charmed us. These Dutch people told us that they could never satisfactorily use Sumatrans for servants. In all the *pasangrahans*

Javanese were used instead. The Sumatrans, we were told, would not take orders as readily and were too independent, while the Javanese were models of submissiveness and trustworthiness.

The natives in this part of Sumatra were still unspoiled. They had seen few white people in their lives and hardly ever a tourist. We found them to be so shy they often ran away when they saw us. So far, the Dutch had not succeeded in thoroughly exploiting this part of the island. The thick jungles and the independent spirit of the people had hindered the inroads of the colonial plantation that had made such headway in Northern Sumatra.

When it began to rain in one palm-shaded lane, we sped to get under the roof of a native hut. An old woman came out, smiled, and talked in Sumatran dialect. She gave us a colorful-hand-woven mat to sit upon and insisted that we use it and not sit on the bare wooden platform.

We returned to the R. R. station on a road which took us through a forest of coconut palms and bamboo huts raised on stilts. It was typical of the many scenes we had experienced since entering Sumatra.

We crossed the R. R. tracks and explored the opposite side of the village. We walked through a large kampong of thatched huts and palms. The women ran into their huts when they saw us coming, and then peeked down at us from a corner of their window or doorway. We peeped into some of the huts. They were clean and neat, although the rooms contained no furniture.

We came upon a jail. The native guard showed us an experimental grove of *cinchona* (or quinine) trees growing in front of the jail. Rocks solidly covered the soil around the trees to keep weeds from growing. The Dutch government had started experimenting with growing quinine-producing trees. Java had grown large plantations of cinchona for years and Sumatra, too, had an untapped source of that wealth.

We left Sumatra at its southern-most tip called Oosthaven with a lingering feeling of regret. This steaming, earthly paradise of tiger grass, jungles, orangutans, panthers, and exotic tropical fruits had made a lasting impression upon us. These lovable, unspoiled natives have been most refreshing to our spirits.

Oosthaven

We had traveled across the great eastern end of Sumatra by train and entered Southaven, our casting off port on our way to Java. After getting off the train, we had a lengthy walk to the boat with our knapsacks. Inasmuch as Kane and Lee spoke no Dutch, the task of smoothing the way always fell to Joe. He had to be the spokesman for us. We had fourth, or deck-class tickets having purchased them along with our train tickets at the R. R. station in Palembang. The tickets were second-class on the train and fourth-class on the boat for the four of us.

We hurried to the boat with light hearts hoping we would be early so as to get a good place. But our hearts sank into our boots when we saw the mob of natives going aboard. Like a colony of ants, they filled up every inch of the deck space. We put our luggage down near the boat and decided to wait a bit until the natives had gone on. But, there was no end to them. There were Malays of all descriptions, from Sumatra and Java, surrounded by their mats, pillows, packs, trunks, bags, bundles, baskets of odorous fruit, and bundles of sugar cane, and coconuts. There wasn't any more room on the boat, and yet, they kept pouring on. We wondered if we should enter on the deck-class gangplank that looked fit only for cargo, or should we go up, bravely, via the *white*-railed first-class gangplank? We chose the latter, and took our belongings resolutely in hand and ascended the upper deck.

Joe, being the official spokesman, went to the first officer and, in Dutch, explained to him that we were looking for material and atmosphere for literary items, and wanted to be with the natives traveling deck-class. This officer didn't like the idea, but he consented for the boys to do so. Tonia, however, had to change to second-class accommodations. The officer gave the boys a special place on the forward deck, where the deck-hands slept.

Near the stern of the boat, on a lower deck, was the small second-class compartment just large enough in which to turn around. The atmosphere was frigid and stiff, like on the K.P.M. Plancius. Only one Dutch boy went in that class; all others were various mixtures of half-caste Dutch and Malayan putting on silly and affected airs.

Joe had to pay the native officials extra for Tonia's second-class ticket, of course. But, on top of it, he had to pay a fine because he did not buy the second-class ticket at the office site near the boat landing. The officer didn't mention that Joe could have gotten it at the office. It was a most unpleasant and nasty management. After arranging deck passage, the boys left the boat and walked to the tiny village, of a half a dozen tiny shops, to buy some supper. It was already dark and they could hardly see what to buy, but they came away with some cookies and bananas. When they returned to the boat, they slipped into Tonia's compartment where they put their cameras and knapsacks, and left six bananas on the bunk. But, alas, those bananas turned out to be the puckery kind, like green persimmons. The voyage was so rocky, that dinner or no dinner, it made no difference.

We had discovered in our short time in the tropics that there are several varieties of bananas. Some, which look so fat and beautiful from the outside, turned out to be rank tasting. These were always fried or roasted by the natives and tasted like delicious fruity sweet potatoes. But the good-eating bananas we found to be delicious. Although Joe and I rarely ate bananas at home, we certainly learned to like them here in the tropics. Here, bananas are at their best and have a fine flavor.

The deck, arranged for the boys, was full of cinders, and in the morning they looked like stokers. They were cold during the night as a stiff wind blew. Joe slept close to Kane and they warmed each other. Joe awoke several times during the night and watched the tropical waters.

The boat went slowly and stopped often. Before sunrise we watched the approach to Merak as we passed several fine-looking islands. A vivid, lush-green, tropical color covered Java's coast.

The first officer seemed glad to see us leave the boat. Dutch officials were very unfriendly and snobbish. White passengers on the K.P.M. Line never go deck class. We insisted on having our way, and the boys went this second time as deck passengers in spite of official opinion, and we had the satisfaction of laughing at Dutch haughtiness.

Merak, Java

A vivid, green circle of mountains enclosed the bay at Merak, and the early morning tropical air made it even more beautiful. However, there was no village there—just the boat-landing, a small K.P.M. office, and the railway station. The train was waiting.

There were two third-classes on trains in Java. One was for the *islanders* or natives, and one for whites and natives who are willing to pay the extra fare.

The Malays were very clean. We found no time when we were offended or annoyed by unpleasant and dirty surroundings in the third-class coaches. This was quite unlike what we had found in China and in cities such as Singapore. At times, the third-class coaches were uncomfortable, having plain long benches and no good shade protection from the sun, but never were they dirty. I would describe them as uncomfortable, hard, and too hot.

Many times, local trains had no extra third-class seats for whites, but still we, as whites, had to pay the extra fare as all whites must buy third-class *witte kaartjes* white cards. The islander's cards were green-colored.

A father and son were in our car. The father spoke no Dutch, but he was proud to show off his embarrassed son who knew some Dutch from school. They were all very kind to us, and we hated to see them leave the train before we reached Batavia. Another couple, who spoke a few words of Dutch, offered us some of their coffee. They bought cooked eggs from a vendor and offered some to us. We gave an American penny to the little boy, and we bought pineapple and puckery chicos from a vendor standing outside the window. They gave us the name of a Chinese hotel in Batavia, and before they left, we had a hearty hand shake all around.

Batavia, Java

The scenery in Batavia was much like a tropical Japan. Every inch of cultivated land was terraced into fields for rice, cocoa, bananas, rubber, and coconuts. There were water buffalo grazing, pulling plows, with naked boys on their backs. It seemed that every native toiled away. They didn't seem as happy as the Sumatrans or as carefree either. The contrast between the cultivated Java and the Sumatran wilderness was striking.

Batavia's railroad station was a new concrete and steel structure built with modernistic lines. It was spacious, airy, and cool. We left our baggage and went out into the old town. We first went to the steamship company to arrange passage to Saigon, and then to the bank to change some money into guilders. Meanwhile, we kept on the lookout for a hotel.

Batavia gave the impression of a small, cramped town. We passed over many bridges and canals. Certain scenes along the canals, with Dutch style building on the banks, made us think we were in Holland. The canals were dirty, filled with native bamboo craft and Dutch-style boats poled by Malays.

After having found the steamship office and bank, we stopped at a small Chinese hotel near the R.R. station, but quickly got out as it was a filthy, bug-infested place. Kane and Lee went to get a square meal in a Chinese restaurant while we two went back to the station. In the second-class refreshment room, we ordered biscuits and soda water. We ate our own hard boiled eggs and some bread. We paid extra for ice water there. Good drinking water had to be prepared and is therefore scarce. The fans circulated and cooled the air.

The little Chinese waiter spoke Dutch so Joe obtained information about hotels. When the boys returned, we set out to find one. The Chinese section of the city, with its hustle and bustle, was a lively contrast to the other parts. We saw scores of Chinese restaurants from the tiniest joints to the most fashionable three-storied chop suey houses. And there was no end to Chinese hotels. The proprietors were surprised to see whites come to them for rooms. We rejected many hotels until we finally came to the newest, largest, and most modern of Chinese hotels—built of concrete and three stories high. The proprietor had a Javanese wife, and although we surprised them at first by coming to their place, they made a reasonable bargain and became friendly and pleasant. Our rooms were on the top floor next to the roof gardens. Clean and neat baths were on the second floor. As customary, tea was included in our room rate, but coffee and bread with butter was an extra we had not expected.

The hotel bath, a tank of clean cold water and a dipper, was the usual tropical bath. There was a wood lattice platform placed over a concrete floor. We poured buckets of water over ourselves, which was mighty refreshing in that sticky hot climate. The hotel also furnished wooden Chinese clogs for the shower. Another convenience was an iron over hot charcoal made available for the laundry. The roof had a water tap, where we did our laundry. Kane had all his clothes draped over the balustrade one day and he had to wear his bathing suit until his clothes dried.

This Chinese section of Batavia was typical of the several cities we have visited. From our vantage point, we could look down on the various activities taking place in the street below and watch lives unfold. The street teemed with the loud noises of phonograph records, loud talking and the general business activity of the vendors.

Finding appropriate food was a problem, so Joe and Lee went on an expedition to purchase food since Lee had learned quite a bit of Malay. But some evenings, they would walk their legs off among tiny Chinese shops and markets to find a *brood* bakery or some canned goods or fruit. It was harder to bargain with the Chinese than it was with the Malays. Other evenings they would go into Chinese restaurants and order hot dishes to bring up to the hotel. There would be fried eggs, hot rice, etc., packed neatly in banana leaves. We made delicious suppers in our hotel room with tea supplied by the management.

The town was lit by electricity, and at night we could see the street transformed as lights from theaters and restaurants came alive for business. The restaurants were busiest at night. Hundreds of small stalls, lit by pitch lamps, opened up on the street around the hotel. Some venders sold coffee, others fruits, cool drinks, or peanuts. We meandered through these stalls, sometimes dressed in kimonos, and leisurely let the cooling breezes fan us as we lounged on the balcony and watched the life below.

In one section of Batavia were the city hall and other old government buildings. The city was generally clean and had many small gardens, but it still had a stiff look. There was no style or beauty in their architecture. Shops, stores and private dwellings were built in typical European style. We found bookstores, apothecaries, bookbinders, and chemists tucked in private dwellings, just as American doctors had offices in their homes.

Hordes of Malay and European office workers came into Batavia each morning on an electric train from Weltevreden. This reminded us of a suburban influx of workers each day in some American cities.

The Dutch had one principle group of colonies in the Dutch East Indies, and they knew how to utilize them. They watched over these islands like a man watches over the '*apple of his eye.*' They were exceedingly cautious about admitting anyone to their islands, and did not like having foreigners do business there. The Chinese, who were the principle business people of the Orient, had to pay heavy taxes to the Dutch government in order to do business there.

Like all other nations, the Dutch government had one reason to have colonies, and that was to make money. In order to get the most from her colonies, the Dutch had turned the colonies into an agricultural paradise; but as a consequence, they had reduced the natives to the lowest stage of poverty. The natives of Java worked very hard, and many of them could not even buy rice as their main diet, but had to buy corn instead. High taxes and general exploitation forced the people to cultivate every inch of their ground while they worked as hard as they possibly could.

The Dutch were a clean and orderly people, and it was only natural that they would introduce their methods to their colonies. Many tourists visiting the islands were convinced the Dutch had found the ideal method of colonization. To our eyes, the Dutch East Indies looked like a toy garden, especially Java, which was so clean and perfect. But, when we looked closer, we found a welling spirit of discontent against Dutch rule.

It is true the Dutch colonizing methods were different from that of the English. They appeared to be more democratic with the natives. They did not draw as strong class lines as the English. They freely intermarried. While they treated the natives delicately, the natives had to suffer before they discovered the main purpose of the Dutch was financial and exploitive.

The Javanese were a beautiful people and we felt sorry for them. We saw them toil away and get nothing in return. In some sections they were so poor they wore only tatters. We asked ourselves continually, "Where does the wealth of these beautiful islands go?" The islands were so rich and orderly, yet the people were so poor.

The Dutch were good bluffers, but the bluff did not work forever. They had allowed the Sultans of Solo and Djokya to rule for effect, but the natives had to pay for the lie inasmuch as they had to pay taxes not only to the Dutch, but also to the Sultan, which allowed the Sultans to maintain their elaborate households and palaces.

Weltevreden, Java

An old-fashioned steam-engine train went between Weltevreded and Batavia. The engine was square and steamed away like it was on fire. It jumped, wobbled and tooted as it rolled along pulling the little coaches. Joe remembered the same kind of steam trains were used in Holland when he lived there. There was one running between The Hague and Schevengingen that Joe used with a monthly pass when he lived in Scheveningen and went to a German school in The Hague.

The town was beautifully laid out with a garden residential section. The houses where foreigners lived were built for comfort in the tropics and had large verandahs, windows, and open courtyards. There were tree-lined, paved streets, gardens, many park squares, and long boulevards for pleasant walking. One long street which was the business street was divided in the middle by a canal. The water in the canal was muddy yellow. The natives walked down concrete steps, which appeared at regular intervals, laundered their clothes, and bathed in the water. It was a picturesque sight to see them beating their folded wet sarongs on the stone steps.

Weltevreden was on higher ground than Batavia, and therefore much healthier. We saw a park square where Dutch soldiers played soccer. The buildings were white concrete or stucco throughout the town. There were large hotels, built like rambling, awning-shaded bungalows which was a beautiful setting amid luxuriant tropical vegetation. The people had many opportunities to create beauty in these tropics with the flowering trees aflame against the vivid greens everywhere.

We bought fruits and cakes for lunch from a native vendor, and ate as we approached the museum. I remember crossing the street at midday, and how I ran fast to shade my head from the terrible rays of that tropical sun. It was unbearable!

On the way to the museum, we entered a large curio shop to get an idea of Javanese crafts and arts. We were delightfully surprised to see objects of fine workmanship and design. We saw many beautiful daggers with handles of precious wood. They used to be the aristocratic weapon of the Javanese gentlemen, and were still worn by the guards of the sultans at Solo and Djokja. There we found materials woven by Balinese and Sumatran women, gold jewelry, carved wooden boxes, buffalo hide *waijang*[8] shadow figures, and batik-materials of silk and cotton. The shop looked like a museum. Some other shops in Weltevreden didn't look business-like at all as they were located in private dwellings with huge advertising signboards on the fences.

The museum was as cool as a refrigerator. There was a large collection of coins in one room. The Chinese had introduced their coins to Java and Bali but they were not used anymore. However, in Bali, the Chinese coins were still legal tender among the natives. The museum displayed the Chinese *Tael*, which was a silver coin known as a "shoe," and had a distinct weight and value. In the "Treasure Room," we found royal jewelry from various islands. The island of Bali and Lombok represented the most beautiful work, while the islands of Borneo and Madura were represented with good goldsmith work. The intricate designs were gorgeous. The Treasury room on the second floor was guarded like a bank for it contains marvels of goldsmiths' and silversmiths' art.

We saw collections of statues from Buddhist and Hindu temples and crafts relative to the family life in all parts of the East Indies. There was wonderful gold and silver work from Bali and other islands as well as interesting collections of weapons. The jewelry showed a distinct Hindu influence. There were displays of hand-woven batik and gold leaf appliquéd materials. The visit to the museum gave us a broad idea of what we could find in the East Indies.

We wanted to purchase some curios but found, to our chagrin, that everything was closed between one and four P.M. This period of three and a half to four hours was tropical siesta time during the heat of the day.

After leaving the museum, we found our way to the tourist bureau where we inquired about Bali, tours in Java, and transportation, etc. We found we knew more than the person in charge! It was a tiny office and looked like a private auto garage and was, in fact, headquarters for the Java Auto Association.

There were many barracks and officers' bungalows in Weltevreden nestled midst shaded parks and lanes. One general feature of Dutch houses was the large floor lamps with red silk shades. These lamps were used inside as well as on the verandahs. The color kept away mosquitoes.

These Dutch were much like the English in their colonies. They do no work themselves but had it attended to by native servants. We saw one fat, elderly Dutch woman come out of a department store in Weltevreden, and behind her trailed a native man servant carrying one minute package for her, two cubic inches in size. It looked so comical we had to burst out laughing. That same woman in Holland would have carried her own package.

One of the main dishes of the Dutch East Indies was called *nasi gorent* (fried rice). The Chinese cooks were expert in making it. It was usually served in combination with ham, pork, chicken, or shrimp and egg, and was served very hot and well-seasoned, piled up high on a dish.

Depok

It was a long journey to Buitenzorg. Early in the morning the train stopped at the little village of Depok. We found the picturesque tree-shaded village full of activity. There were a few Dutchmen in pajamas, and sandals standing in their gardens. Small children were on their way to school at 7:00 A.M. Running through the village was a clean canal lined by beautiful great trees and streets. The canal had bamboo bridges crossing here and there with a quiet path running along the bank.

The natives came into town in one long procession, for half a mile or more, carrying loaded baskets on their balanced poles slung across their shoulders. The baskets were filled with beautiful fruit common to these islands. We saw our first beggars here. There may have been three of them.

Everything was neat and orderly. There were great piles of rice in large flat, round fiber trays, three to four feet across, and huge piles of freshly dug and washed peanuts. There were no bad smells. There were piles of roots and vegetables on little tables. Clean cheeses were displayed on fresh banana leaves, and cooked foods were served in woven banana leaf containers or in small clean dishes.

Portable restaurants, with low bamboo benches which were about two inches off the ground, and the Chinese bowls gave a Lilliputian feel to this restaurant scene. The charcoal brazier and kitchen department was clean, neat and compact. These people were so neat that we would not have hesitated to eat off their tables or from their bowls. Only we could not be so sure in what sort of water the food had been washed, since often it was contaminated. Everyone ate with his hands. We remarked that the Dutch might do a flourishing business in knives and forks once they taught the natives to use them.

Market women wore shawls and much more jewelry than the Sumatran women we had seen. The vendors, both men and women, were very kind to us. Had we known their language, they would have gladly conversed with us and told us all we wished to know about their products. We noticed one solid white mass resembling cottage cheese, but found out it was tofu, a product made from soybeans, and used extensively here and in Japan and China. The vendor offered to give us a taste.

These people also bargained, but it was not as obnoxious as in some other Oriental lands. They asked more than the price should be, of course, but the buyer offered less and a speedy and agreeable compromise was made in a friendly manner with little time lost.

We remained there for over an hour, and then caught the train again to go on to Buitenzorg. We saw well-cultivated land everywhere with terraced rice fields all around. It looked like a tropical Japanese countryside with the orderliness of the Swiss or Dutch.

We found Buitenzorg to be a beautiful city, but a typical tourist town. The pettiness of taxi boys and children asking for money was annoying. The city was a garden of tree-shaded paved streets lined with neat bungalows and surrounded by mountains and fields, all of which could be viewed from the kampongs. Much of the scene, including the river, could be viewed from the balcony of our Hotel Belleview. The scenery reminded us of an intermingling of Mexico and Switzerland.

The town was beautifully laid out with tall kanari trees lining the streets. Chimes and bells rang every quarter hour from tall belfries and church towers. It seemed that all towns in Java had clock chimes, either in the square, or in the churches, and in private homes. We felt the atmosphere was as a prim bourgeois village life laid out along Dutch lines. This town was the residence of the Dutch Governor General.

Here, again, there were children riding bicycles and little one-horse carriages with clanging bells. Javanese coolies, carrying great loads on their shoulders, trotted along the streets. The contrast was great between the brilliant sarongs of the upper-class Javanese and the nakedness of the coolies.

We enquired from some children about where to find the botanical gardens. On our way there, we came upon a museum devoted to the commercial products of the islands. We spent quite some time looking with stereoscopic machines, through which the use of glass photo plates revealed the various processes of native products on the islands. As we turned a handle, a new scene would turn up. The whole process of tin mining, making sugar, turpentine, cocoa, kapok, tea, coffee, fiber for straw hats was shown. We also found vegetables, preserved in alcohol that had been grown on the island. There were cases of native ebony wood, and products like canes, boxes, hair and clothes brush tops.

Then we toured the zoological museum which displayed extraordinary types of stuffed beautiful birds and animals found in the Indies — herons, egrets, and birds of paradise. We saw a skeleton of a giant whale that had been washed ashore on Java after a terrific storm. It was eighty feet long and had weighed about seven thousand pounds.

Finally, we came to the botanical gardens, founded in 1817, and the Governor General's house which was in the middle of the gardens. The garden was cut through by the rushing Ijiliwong River dividing the garden into an older section and a newer one. We walked the famous Kanari Avenue lined with giant kanari trees and bedecked with a great variety of climbing orchids, fine fern palms, and parasite plants hanging from the upper branches. There was a lily pond with giant Victoria Regis lotuses and many varieties of water plants. There were little pavilions and rest houses placed at convenient and scenic points, and special orchid houses with hundreds of varieties. They even had a carnivorous plant which devoured flies and insects. Bamboo-canopied lanes, with every variety of tropical tree and bush, were carefully tended and labeled. Nearly every tree and plant was different from its neighbor.

A delightful walk took us to the rushing Tjiliwong River. Crowds of little naked boys and girls splashed and bathed while the women washed clothing and bathed in the water. Here we came across two small Javanese girls who were merrily gathering butternuts. They offered us some and, at the same time, looked over their shoulders to see if any watchman detected them. They followed us until we sat down in a pavilion. They gave us nuts, which we accepted. They then asked for pennies, but were looking out for the guard. We couldn't crack the nuts, until we received a stone fetched by the little girls, then we succeeded.

Little Javanese girls looked so cute, because they looked like miniature women, wearing the same kind of sarong and jacket. Their skirts were long, and their bare feet pattered beneath. As we passed through the kampong, a bevy of cute little girls asking for money appeared out of every yard.

On this long street, in front of the Garden entrance, was a single row of shops. We went in one and purchased some photos. Buitenzorg is climatically an ideal place since it is situated on a high plateau and didn't get the oppressive damp heat. As a whole, it gave the impression of a mountain resort town. We felt sorry as we thought that in a few days we were to leave this high plateau of Java to descend again into the warm, moist valleys of its hot coastal regions.

In the government pawnshop we looked at almost every pawned sarong but found nothing we liked well enough to buy. Besides, we didn't know enough about Javanese batik as yet to be able to judge a good piece from a print.

We walked on through town and back to the railroad station seeking a place for lunch. Plenty of natives crowded around watching us. We found a clean Chinese restaurant where a small eight year-old fellow, served us. He spoke Dutch, and had a most gracious manner and a big smile. He stood on a chair to reach napkins in a cupboard, took down a clean menu, and explained the Malay words on the menu. When words failed, he brought us the item itself. Once he brought us a shrimp, then a can of peas, a bit of raw meat, and potatoes. Joe purchased a pound of Edam cheese from a store across the street, and we all had dinner. It poured rain while we were eating; but after it cleared; we went back to the train station and caught the train for further points east in Java.

Buitenzorg to Sukabumi

The glorious scenery of swift winding rivers, mountains and ravines was similar to but more beautiful than Mexico because of the highly cultivated land. It was a medley of palms, bananas, and mountain ranges. It was lovelier than Japan because of its rich tropical coloring. Here we found the highest state of cultivation amid a glorious panorama of scenery.

The terraced rice paddies, with their complicated irrigation systems, were a marvelous sight especially at the time when rice was still young. Water in the terraced fields glistened in the sun as it poured from one level into another like little waterfalls. The contours of the hillsides made beautiful patterns as they were backed with the brilliant pea-green of the hills, yellow and brown of ripe rice, and the kapok trees and beneath which were neat little tea bushes.

We passed deep ravines and rushing rivers with lush vegetation almost hiding the river below. We saw frail-looking, but strong native bamboo bridges spanning streams. Most of the rivers were reddish color from the soil they carried along. The sudden and daily rains made the rivers always swift, swirling around boulders and rocks along the way.

Volcanic mountains in the distance, cultivated banana plantations, and the endless variety of palms enriched the view. Some palms had white trunks and skimpy topknots and were usually found in clusters. There were giant papaya trees often with two or three branching trunks. Here and there, we saw a patch of corn, peanuts or pole beans but most of the land was contoured in rice paddies. The ground was constantly damp in the rainy season but never disagreeable or cold.

The little railroad station on Tijurug was like a gem sitting amidst high, dark-blue mountains on one side along a narrow, swift river and glorious vegetation on the other. This was a good example of a west Java agricultural village.

We arrived at Sukabumi towards evening. It was Joe's and Lee's job to find a hotel since Kane, sporting a long black beard and wearing shorts, was too conspicuous. From our dress, anybody could see that we were not ordinary tourists. So, Kane and Tonia remained at the train station while the other two went to try their luck. The boys went to many hotels but found all asked too high prices, so they kept searching. They always looked for the impossible — a clean, unpretentious hotel with reasonable rates, — and they usually managed to find it.

They agreed upon a certain price at the Juliana Hotel in spite of the native manager's protestations. Joe was a real bargainer. He showed them how many rooms they had empty in their hotel, and told them we could take two rooms; therefore, the manager should give them to us for what Joe offered. As a rule, we paid Florin 1 (or $2.00) per room which included breakfast with coffee, bread and butter, and tea during the day. But when we left the next morning, the manager made a scene. We lent him no ear, paying him only the agreed price and we went to the station.

Sukabumi's business section at night was quite lively. The noise, lights, and activity reminded us of Japan. Phonograph music blared out from every shop. While we waited for our supper on the second floor of the Shanghai café, we looked at the busy nightlife below, and killed funny little ants which scurried over the stained tablecloth.

This city had the look of a Swiss resort. Many hotels and pensions built in a semi-Swiss style seemed fitted for the tropics. They were surrounded by mountain ranges with hilly and winding streets and brooks rushing under bridges. Each new city on this mountain plateau was lovelier than the last. The air was splendid and cool and healthier than that of the coastal regions. The urge to walk and breathe revived again, and we wouldn't have minded if we could have remained many months. The altitude was about 2,300 feet; population 23,500, of which about 13,000 were Europeans and Eurasians.

The Juliana Hotel was near the train station. It had a large balcony underneath wide eaves, and a rushing river beyond the garden. Pigeon houses, coconut, bananas, and blooming jasmine trees in the garden completed the tranquil scene. It was a Malayan hotel and was clean and comfy.

On the square we saw our first Javanese-Mohammedan Mosque, called *aloon.* The structure gave a pleasing impression being simple, dignified, and devoid of ornamentation. There were no minarets which characterize other mosques. It had raised polished-marble floors inside, and a roof supported with many pillars. No altar or idols were seen. We left our shoes outside. There was a place for natives to wash their feet before entering. People knelt facing Mecca and silently prayed. Natives were pleased to show us around.

In Sukabumi, there were many Chinese and Japanese shops, beauty parlors, schools and movie houses. There was more auto traffic than in Batavia. We lost our way back to the hotel and, on dark streets, wandered for an hour past native vendors and stands with strange-smelling fruit. At last, we found our way back, slept like dead ones, and the next morning caught the train for Tjiaudjur.

Tjiaudjur

We arrived in Tjiaudjur at about nine-thirty A.M. Trains in Java didn't run at night, but started at four-thirty to five A.M. to avoid the heat. The journey necessitated sleeping in a Javanese town. This small town was like many other mountain resorts, as far as beauty goes, but without many hotels.

There was the usual muddy river rushing through the village. The rivers of Java are not large but they seem always to be full of water, as if just after a cloudburst. We walked a circle about the town beneath tall canopies of trees along narrow roads bordered by picturesque bungalows. We met three Europeans and a priest. We exchanged greetings and went on our way. Coming back, we found the main auto highway which connected to other towns. On this road were large Dutch residences, a bank, and schools. All this was set in a leafy rural setting. Further along was the green square *aloon*, and the Mohammedan mosque or *missegit*. We heard a deep sounding wood-and-hide drum which called the people to prayer.

In the market, we discovered a greater richness of produce and bounty of household articles than any other market we had seen in Java. Since this village was located in a more moderate clime, many varieties of vegetables were available: carrots, tomatoes, beets, potatoes, etc. We tried a piece of jackfruit which was not bad, but was not really tasty either. The market had a picturesque display of food. Most of the vendors had their wares on cloths spread on the floor. We wanted more and more to walk around the stalls. We did not seem to get enough of it. This village was full of coconuts and copra drying on trays in front of the shops. We saw two jackfruits in front of a market that were as large as pigs. We saw cocoa bean trees and coconuts for the first time. Cabbages seemed to be a specialty. There was a restaurant on poles, in which customers were served while sitting on woven mats on the floor. As usual, the retail, wholesale, provision, and merchandise shops were owned by Chinese.

We were used to walking several hours every day. The tropical heat bothered us very little. We developed a system of covering the whole village, from one end to the other, in the least possible time. We developed a sharp sense of smell which led us to the most important sections of the town. We walked about the places in our usual conspicuous way. Our dress told the people we were not regular tourists. What tourists walked? They always used autos! It was Kane, especially, who drew the attention of people. Children would run away when they saw his long, black beard. We saw women point to his beard and show an expression of fright, or disgust. The Javanese men had hardly any beard.

Padalarang

Here, were some of the finest rice terraces in the West Indies. We saw remarkable engineering feats, with whole mountains cut down into winding terraces and undulating contours of paddies, with water flowing from one level to another, various brilliant greens of new rice shoots, and sunlight glistening on the water. It was an unforgettable sight.

We saw workers in the paddies, weeding or planting, standing in mud above their knees. Java is such a fertile country, it was sad to think that most of the profits went not to the natives who toil like slaves, but to the Dutch to increase their capital.

Bandung

We left our knapsacks at the station's parcel room, and the four of us walked to town. We asked policemen and soldiers for the way to the largest hotel. We wanted to find out whether there were busses to Garut, since to go by train we would have to double back and go a much longer route.

Bandung was situated on the plain of Bandung at an altitude of 2,300 feet. The population was 155,000 of which about 11,000 were Europeans and Eurasians. The climate was healthy and bracing, and it was one of the most prosperous parts of Java. The surrounding mountains were volcanic. Most were dormant, but some were active. This was the third largest city in Java, and one of the loveliest. There was a Dutch military garrison here and, also, the only Technical University in the Netherlands.

Many Japanese dry goods shops were in business here. The merchants sat on a raised floor and showed wares, something like the shops in Japan. Every section produced its own designs in batik which were handed down from generation to generation. We heard Dutch spoken here more than in any other city visited so far. It was a lively city with students and many natives.

We learned there was a Japanese-owned bus company which had a bus to Garut. They were especially nice to us when they heard we had been to Japan and liked their country. They reserved four front seats for us, and gave us a map that showed excursions we could take from Garut. They took our tickets and sent for our knapsacks. However, we still had hours before the bus would leave, so we roamed around in the city. Tonia went into an ice cream parlor, while Joe went to the Japanese photographer. All over the Dutch East Indies the Japanese had beautiful hair-dressing establishments and photo shops. We bought some food and had our lunch on the bus.

The ride between Bandung and Garut was a beautiful experience. We got a close view of Javanese agriculture. Rice paddies were in all stages of cultivation. Men were chopping up muddy soil, plowing with buffalo, and setting out new rice shoots on irrigated steep slopes which graced each view. Each new view put the last one to shame. Some terraces, on these steep slopes, were no wider than one and a half to two feet. The road was excellent, winding through the mountains and passing many native villages. Some people came to the bus stop to see who had arrived and who had departed. Some small, naked children stood by and looked on. We had a good driver, steady and level-headed. There really was a shortage of buses in Java.

*****

The city of Garut is much like other towns we have visited situated on a high plateau, it had a scenic Swiss-like atmosphere. It was a town of about 30,000 people and seemed to have more farmers in its population than businessmen. The city was the business center for west Java batik, and also for craftsmen who also made fine grass and fiber mats, baskets and hats.

*****

We stayed at the Madika Hotel which was as clean as a pin with tiles glistening and marble topped tables and chairs all around. In the open corridors were masses of blooming orchids hanging from moss and bark pieces. We were surprised at the sumptuous breakfast served to us the next morning. We had two breakfasts settings of eggs, bread and butter, jam, cheese, and coffee and milk. We took a motor car to the little village of Tjisurupan at the foot of the volcano, Papandayan. Again, we were treated with an "up-close" look at a Javanese village and farm life. The road was paved and smooth. The natives were harvesting grain by hand. On their backs they carried great bunches of the golden heads held in place by cotton sarong scarves or tied to the ends of bamboo poles. The air became cooler here, almost chilly. We could see the center of the volcano since the crater was on the side of the mountain rather than centered on the top.

A huge, expensive resort hotel sat on a ledge overlooking the plain. Garut and all the mountains could be seen from this vantage point. The village was actually smaller than the hotel grounds. We took time for an extended hike of a few miles through a bamboo forest trail, but we did not have enough time to hike to the crater. We regretted that we had not started earlier in the morning. We wanted to stay overnight and hike the next morning, but there was no place to stay except the resort hotel, and it was too expensive.

While resting on the trail in the bamboo forest, we became aware for the first time of the creaking and rattling of bamboo in the wind. It was a weird and uncanny sound, like bones being jiggled together. The creak and groan made us believe they were snapping or breaking as if in an earthquake. We were at about 4,200-foot elevation, and the air felt like that in Nikko, Japan. On our way down, we saw processions of natives from the fields carrying their loads of ripe rice to be threshed.

We arrived back at Garut in time to take the afternoon train to Wanaradja. This proved to be one of those learning exercises encountered when traveling. We arrived at the train stop, got off and started to walk to the village, which was quite some distance from the R.R. station. Along with us, walked the homecoming villagers and we seemed to be leading the way through the rice paddy fields. No other people were around except the natives, for no other people seemed to come to this place as tourists. We intended to visit a mountain kampong called Papandak, but we found it was twelve kilometers round trip. We would have climbed it, but there was absolutely no place to stay overnight on Papandak, or in Wanaradja. The natives told us we would find hotels in Garut, which we had just left. There was not even a Malayan or Chinese inn. "Nothing!" The whole village turned out to follow us back to the R.R. station gazing as if we were from Mars. We took the next train, which left about an hour after we had arrived. We journeyed until after dark to the small village of Tasikmalaja, which had a hotel. We learned nothing about this town, since we arrived late and left before dawn. We found a small Malayan hotel run by a family who chewed betel nuts, and a boy of about fifteen who spoke Dutch. Our rooms were just big enough for a bed and mosquito netting. There was a woven palm-mat floor and ceiling which was whitewashed. Also, there was in the yard next to some ducks, the usual concrete tank with a dipper to pour water over ourselves. We took a stroll after dark and, further on, found quite a few more hotels and a Dutch Concordia Club. Joe went in to get information regarding bus or motor connections between Nonosobo and Borobudur.

There was one not very exciting movie house so we came back to the hotel, had some tea and went to bed, instructing the boy to call us at four A. M. The little hotel had about four chiming clocks so, we awoke before being called. We gulped hot coffee and bread and butter, served by a little sleepy-eyed boy, and went to the station. The train pulled out at four fifty-eight A.M. while the city was still dark

Leaving this village, we passed the last mountain station and good scenery. The train rushed through lowland rubber plantations and swampy marshes where giant trees were rooted in black-stagnant water. The landscape was even less prosperous looking. The crops we saw changed from corn back to coconuts, bananas and sugarcane. The appearance of the natives and the villages were poorer and less thriving than in middle Java.

The air became stickier and warmer as we traveled lower into a monotonous landscape! We made no stops on this eleven-hour trip. We purchased duck eggs, rice, salt, and a few bananas for lunch. Some school children on the train were very curious, as they watched us. Over all, it was a tiresome, hot, and dirty journey.

We began to see strange, roofed-bamboo carts painted in gay colors and drawn by powerful bullocks and humped sacred cows. These were the native carts of this section. The bullocks were yoked to crude wooden harnesses. The roofs of the houses in the villages were tall with a squared-off peak and had thatched or tiled roofs. The colors of the costumes were somber, most often just indigo blue. The natives were much darker-skinned and wore big Chinese hats while working in the fields.

Djokja Karta

We arrived in Djokja Karta at four-fifteen P.M. in a downpour that cooled the air. We waited awhile and then set out for the Djokja Hotel and prepared to stay for four days. The town was filled with hordes of natives clad in shabby dark-blue sarongs and carrying baskets of produce on their backs. We found them sitting on sidewalks, at little stands, selling all manner of foods and trinkets or trudging about with baskets swinging from the familiar bamboo pole.

The main street was filled with many Japanese beauty parlors, imported fruit stores, Dutch bakeries, etc. But in spite of all these modern things, the city was essentially Javanese, and we felt we actually were in Java. We noticed particularly the contrast between aristocratic-looking Javanese and the poorest of the poor natives. The men were beautifully dressed in dark sarongs gathered in pleats in front that kicked out like a fan when they walked. They wore dark-striped jackets which were buttoned in the semi-Chinese fashion, batik caps which were tied smartly with a small-peaked straw hat, leather sandals and a cane. Their carriage was stately, never hurried or hasty, yet, not lazy either — just collected and composed their faces serene and calm. We found a fine Chinese restaurant. We dined and then walked back to our hotel for a night's rest after our long journey. We felt we were in a vastly interesting place and looked forward to tomorrow when we would begin to explore.

We set out early in the morning and got a permit to visit the Sultan's Kraton. We tried to find two pandhuises (pawn shops), but got mixed up and wandered along interesting native side-streets near the pasar. Here, we found gold and silversmiths fashioning native jewelry. The streets were blocked by the huge bulk of two-wheeled carts and large yoked-bullock teams. Wrinkled old women, with bedraggled hair and wearing short sarongs, sat selling food from their baskets. They wore a piece of sarong wound around their breasts and no jacket. Many had sores on their legs and all of them had scarlet-stained lips and black teeth. Some had a great wad of shredded tobacco stuck between their lips and gums with half of it protruding from between their lips and hanging on their chins. It was disgusting to see.

As usual, we found ourselves in the market. How does one avoid a visit to the pasar? It was a colorful sight. The long open stands were on a raised platform a foot above a walk of cool-polished granite or smooth tile. Above each station was an individual roof. The pasar covered a city block. Here we saw all that was available, most of which we were familiar, but still there were a few things with which we were not. The women vendors, and their wares, were a kaleidoscope of types and colors. It seemed all of them were smiling and friendly. Raggedly-dressed women with baskets on their backs followed us around and asked to carry our purchases for a few pennies. Huge sluggish horseflies that seem to be native to Djokja swarmed over everything uncovered, especially the meat and bakery things.

In the market we saw a demented native woman who seemed to surprise even the natives. She wore a tattered fiber sack around her waist, her hair was wild and dirty, and she was miserably thin. She jumped and pointed; one minute acting in glee, and then she fell into a melancholy visage. Later, we saw her again on the main street, wildly gesticulating — stopping again and again.

The sound of cowbells was common, as every bullock had one around its neck as it slowly pulled the huge, two-wheeled covered cart along the street. The humps of these beasts wobbled back and forth as they walked and caused the tinkling of their brass bells as their heads swayed in a peaceful rhythm. It was a peaceful medieval picture.

Djokja had a few art shops. In one, native crafts were sold. In another one, a pleasant Eurasian girl, who spoke English, Dutch, and Malay, showed us many items, and explained the processes by which they were made. This shop had native fans, lamp shades, brass wear, fine silver, excellent swords and daggers in rare wood-cases, buffalo-horn spoons, forks, tortoise-shell wares, batik, and tooled buffalo hide *wayan* shadow play figures and woven materials from the island. Javanese art was highly developed, and showed marked Indian and Hindu influence.

Many people in our hotel lived in the small rooms surrounding the courtyard. We had a good opportunity to observe native life there. The Malays were easy-going people, talkative amongst themselves, always laughing and singing to each other and even doing nothing beautifully well. We have yet to hear a Javanese person quarrel. They seem very peaceful. All their songs seemed to be of the same melody, sad and melancholy. Its roots, we think, probably came from Arabic or Hindu music. We saw very little cooking done. Traveling restaurants would set up shop in the courtyard, and people would purchase a penny of rice, a bit of this, and bit of that, and had their meal. The only actual work done, we noticed, had been done by women who were seen now and then sewing or washing. Men were likely to get out of bed at one or two in the early morning, light a pipe and talk as they sat on benches with their feet tucked under them. They slept a great deal during the day.

We went to the theatre or opera twice. The theater, called the *Katoprak*, was a modernized version of Javanese, Arabic, and Turkish motifs mixed together. No classic dances or plays were performed while we were there, since it was a holy month for Mohammeds. It was the time of a forty-day fasting and repenting period before the New Year. They ate no food between noon and six P.M. and during these days, no classical theater was performed.

We did go to the Katoprak two nights. The second night was a continuation of the first. We sat until one A.M. the first night and until twelve P.M. the second. Perhaps the third night was the continuation of the same opera.

The music accompaniment was gamelan music with drums and modern violin. The songs were of low and sad tones. The main characters always chanted their stories to the same melodies. Certain distinct sounds announced the coming on stage of a new character or the departure of another. Characters, who denoted strength, reminded us of Chinese mandarin actors. Apparently they had been influenced by Chinese acting, which we could see in their arm and leg movements upon entering or leaving the stage. The men's costumes were semi-Turkish and ugly, but the women wore beautiful Javanese costumes. Their movements, especially the fingers and hands, were graceful and lovely. The Javanese had a good sense of humor, and the opera featured two good comedians and a third that was a marvel. Not only was he a fine comedian but a natural-born master ballet dancer who could have put to shame many western dancers. His art was in his mastery of pantomime. He was as graceful throwing back his shawl in a bewitching manner, as the Chinese actor Mei Lau Fang (whom we saw in Peking). In half of the play he impersonated a woman. Every turn of his head, or a look, or a movement of his hand spoke. If he was in a European country, he would be a well-known artist with the proper training instead of in a small native open-air theatre in Java.

Just as in the Chinese theatre, the characters of the Katoprak had traditional motions denoting their characters. The voices were not good, but we enjoyed the lovely melodies and the music between acts. Since we did not understand the language, many times we did not laugh with the audience. But, we could readily understand the main comedian just from his pantomime. For a small native theatre, they had a remarkable collection of stage sets and props. The audience was well-behaved. We saw some patrons, the second night, with children sleeping all through the play.

Sultan's Palace

Kraton was a vast area enclosed within the city, like a city within a city. The main gateway faced a large square or outer court where old waringin trees had been clipped and trained into forms of colossal *payangs*, or state umbrellas, as a badge of royalty. Within are many buildings, streets, and walls, which were the quarters for numerous wives, officials, retainers and relatives. The Palace was built for air and comfort. All the buildings had open halls with a raised marble floor, beamed roof, and carved pillars. Antiquated guards stood or squatted about. They wore their hair long and tucked up in a round braid in back of the head, with tall black fez hats. Their uniforms consisted of ornamented sarongs, and dark jackets with beautiful swords in a gold or precious wood case stuck through a wide belt at their back. The guards' living quarters were little roofed halls where they had pillows and matting laid out or rolled up. However, everything looked useless and artificial. There were sixteen visitors who went through with us. One man had to rush back to his hotel and change from his shorts to long trousers since long trousers had to be worn by male visitors. Everything which had belonged to the "Sultan I" was held sacred now —- golden carriage, musical instruments, sedan chair, etc. A small parade of guards passed by playing flutes and drums. None of them carried guns but only their sword or lance. The Sultan was vastly rich, He owned his own sugar plantation and coffee mills, and employed over 1,500 people. Countless loafers and other human parasites filled the palace grounds getting paid for being bored and doing nothing. People in Djokja had to pay taxes to the Sultan too. And the Dutch government gave him a subsidy as well. It will be another two or three generations before the agreement between the Sultan and the Dutch government ends the Sultanate.

Special slabs of marble, raised from the floor, were guarded and polished by kneeling servants. These were the slabs where the Sultan stood or sat. Also, a perpetual light was kept burning beside his royal throne. Guards and servants knelt down and raised clasped hands to their foreheads before they stepped onto the marble floors of the various halls. Architecturally, it was beautifully simple. The main decoration was on carved or painted pillars and roof beams.

Borobudur

We took a motor car to one of Java's great Hindu monuments which dated back to the days when Hinduism was Java's religion. They were probably built in the eighth or ninth century. The temple, the inspiration of Hindu architects and sculptors was erected over part of the ashes of the Buddha, as tradition goes. It was a gigantic structure built around and over a hill. The hill formed the main stupa, enclosed and surrounded by a series of sculptured galleries — four in number. Three terraces rose at the top. The uppermost was a tall, bell-shaped stupa, right in the center, towering above everything. This stupa (*dagoba*), formerly contained an unfinished statue of Buddha. On the top terrace, there were countless bell-shaped mounds each containing a mutilated or a whole statue of a sitting Buddha. From the magnificent vista at the top, we could see mountains, thick coconut forests and rice paddies.

From the first to the fourth gallery, the walls were covered with bas-relief illustrating the various stages in the life of Buddha. Great gargoyle heads served as rain gutters and spouts at each corner, while delicate flowers birds and animals were carved into the gutters. The temple was carved with dark volcanic stone. The action and modeling of the statues and bas-relief carvings were splendid even after all these centuries of erosion. The temple, as a whole, was not a graceful structure, but the details in the decoration were remarkable. One could see the Indian and Hindu influence in the designs.

*****

The building is 531 feet around the base and the carvings set end to end would measure two miles. When the Mohammedans conquered Java, they destroyed all the Hindu Temples, but the Hindu priests of

Borabudur covered their temple with earth and let nature cover it with vegetation. For six hundred years it remained so. In 1814, Raffles, who was then secretary of the East Indies, discovered it around 1907 to 1911, and preserved it as a national Javanese Monument.

*****

Mendut, was a small temple near Muntilau which was not far from Borobudur. We found there, a large and fine statue of Buddha. It was eighteen feet tall and the natives firmly believed that this had been Buddha's actual height.

We went from Djokja to Solo by horse carriage to another group of Hindu Temples called Prambanan. The carriage was antiquated and pulled by two little, nearly-starved horses. A young child acted as footman in back of the carriage. Around this district were many Hindu ruins. Some were mere mounds of stone while others were more preserved. The Prambanan group of temples and altars were not as well preserved as Borobudur but had far more excellent carvings. Not only was there bas-relief, but also complete sculptured pieces. Many of the groups were as fine and exquisitely done as any Greek sculpturing we had seen. Pure Hindu designs predominated, such as the symbolism of the "Tree of Life" with pairs of different birds or animals at its base. We could have spent days viewing the magnificent carvings. Here, we found images of the sacred cow and one altar which was devoted to it. We found flower offerings placed before the images. Pennies, rice, incense, and flowers could be found placed before the statues showing the mixture of Hinduism and Mohammedan religions in Java. Supervised excavations were still going on repairing and reconstructing the altars. Mounds of labeled stones and carvings laid about — enough to build a large temple. The Dutch deserve credit for how well and orderly they recreated and preserved these ancient treasures.

We returned to the station and caught the next train to Solo, which was the seat of the Sultanate of the Sura Karta district. The population was about 135,000 of which about 2,500 are European and Eurasians. The native ruler was called Susuhunan. The Sultan had ninety-nine wives. Only the children of the first wife were honored as princes and princesses. The government paid him a certain amount for the upkeep of his palace, which was longer and more beautiful than the one in Djokja. It was open only on Wednesdays, so we could not see it. In Solo, the sultan was called Sunan. Solo was an interesting and colorful place due to the contrast between wealth and poverty. It seemed there was more poverty here than anywhere we had seen in Java.

At this lower altitude Solo was very hot. We saw enormous drying and fermenting sheds for tobacco throughout the countryside. Very fine sugar cane was grown here too. In Solo, we had another splendid opportunity to study native life. The Sunan seemed more real to us than it was in Djokja. An air of richness and prosperity pervaded wherever the Sunan's property was located. Solo was rated the most progressive city in Java. More natives here dressed in European dress than elsewhere, and the royal family was educated and modern. One of the princes had studied abroad and managed the biggest business in Solo, thus breaking old family traditions.

On one of our long walks to a park, we passed many wholesale batik houses. Solo was a large batik center. We went into one of the wholesale houses, and a younger son, who spoke good English, took us behind the store to the factory to show us how batik was made. The work room was really a sweat shop. Men stood over rolls of white cotton stamping the first design in wax from intricate brass stamps or dies. Some Malay workers were stomping the materials in huge dye vats with their feet, while others were stirring materials in a boiling caldron to boil out the wax. Wax, water and dye ran over the ground everywhere. The second and third waxing were done by hand by women and small girls sitting on the damp ground. Material was held over a wooden rack. A charcoal fire kept a pot of wax molten while they dipped their small copper *Tchanting* instruments into it. Elsewhere, whole ears of corn were being submerged in ashes and charcoal to keep food warm for these workers. They were pitifully paid, working by piecework. The women received less than f.0.5 a day, together with a bit of corn or rice, and fish.

*****

85

The main difference in quality of sarongs is in the dye used. Javanese dyes are very expensive and very good. They will last five years or more and never fade. German dyes are not as good. Cotton can be left in Java dye vats for twenty days with no harm to the fiber. Wood bark and flowers from Shanghai and Singapore are used. Materials can only be left in the vat for one hour, and then must be taken out and dried before putting it in again. Synthetic dyes have acids that weaken the material. German dyes are much cheaper. The wax recipe is: "1 1/2 wax; 1 paraffin; 1 resin; - dry materials out of sun but in a wind."

*****

A Chinese boy accompanied us to Sriwedari, which was an open-air theatre in a lovely little park where classic Javanese drama and dancing could be seen. The dancing was most graceful. The sarongs were worn like a train between the dancer's feet, and they moved with short steps while kicking back the train in a beautiful and graceful manner. Arm and finger movements were lovely and intricate. The orchestra was pure gamelan with many wooden sounds. The melancholy voices and delicate movements of the dancers was pleasing and soothing. Distinct arm movements of throwing the ends of their shawls into the air was beautifully done. Every movement of an arm or finger had symbolic meaning which native audiences understood and readily distinguished between fine or vulgar movements. The dance lasted one hour and was followed by the *wayang* drama until 2:00 A.M. This drama was symbolic too, full of intricate body control and movement often like the finest modernistic dancing. The main actor was a marvel of grace and agility and took his positions swiftly like the most accomplished ballet dancer. We remembered similar movements from the Chinese theatre.

The actors playing in the Sunan's Kraton are, of course, the best though they receive no more pay—only more honor and renown. The first actor gets, at the most, only f3.50 per night. The actors do other work during the day such as batik printing and dying or other labor. Then they act and dance several nights a week. Since the plays last so far into the night, most of the actors eat a cheap form of opium to keep awake. There was more opium in Solo, it seemed, than in the rest of Java.

Traveling street singers, musicians, and dancers roamed about the market places. They set up their drums and gamelan bells and played for poor, ragged crowds as the ballad singers of old used to do. A few pennies were usually their reward. We saw a girl in an outdoor pasar, singing to the women vendors and accompanied by a boy patting a long drum with his palm with weird harmonic beats. At night, we heard many people singing. To hear their chants and music at a distance was an unforgettable experience. The melodies were so haunting they tugged at our hearts.

In Solo, beggars slept on the sidewalks, in corner doorways, under trees, and on steps. The city was not clean and orderly as in other parts of Java. The huge bullock carts were not gaily painted. They looked worn and old. We could have spent more time in Solo, for our interest never lagged in watching native life.

CLASSICAL DANCER --SOLO, JAVA

BOROBUDUR TEMPLE IN JAVA

ON THE RIM OF BROMO VOLCANO, JAVA

RICE TERRACE IN JAVA

DETAIL OF BAS RELIEF @ BOROBUDUR TEMPLE, JAVA

JAVANESE WAYANG DRAMA in SOLO . JAVE

SACRED OXEN CARTS – MIDDLE , JAVA

"SRI BALI" OUTRIGGER FROM JAVA TO BALI

TONIA CROSSED THE RIVER ON
SHOULDERS OF ONE OF THESE MEN
The bridge had been washed out

ENTERTAINMENT IN EVERY BALINESE VILLAGE

TYPICAL VILLAGE STREET IN BALI

Note mud walls covered by straw

DOGS! DOGS! EVERY WHERE

KRISS DANCERS
POSSESSED BY THE EVIL SPIRIT THEY DO NOT
FEEL THE SHARP POINTS OF THE SWORDS--BALI

Modjokerto

We left Solo in the early afternoon and arrived at Modjokerto at night. This was an important sugar center with many sugar factories. It was once the site of the mighty empire of Modjopahi. The village had a small but interesting museum which contained relics dating from the Hindus' occupation. The museum was small and was tended by an old Javanese man. The whole appearance was that of a little building tucked away in a private garden. We were allowed to look at the statues inside and knew that no one would follow or direct us. There was just one room with a side annex. A woman sold flowers at the entrance and we saw these offerings as well as incense and burning sweet-smelling woods placed before the statues. Inside, we saw fine pieces of statuary of pure Hindu origin and also some of pure Javanese origin. Those of the latter were more grotesque. The "Elephant Buddha" appeared in many figures too.

Sleepy canals cut through the village with little native huts on each side. Small bamboo bridges crossed the canal in which ducks swam, and people washed their clothes in the dirty water. There was a large Chinese compound with beautiful mansions and temple grounds.

Our hotel for the night was with a high caste Javanese family in a private pension. All spoke Dutch fluently. There were three children of school age, who were bashful, yet curious. We went in while they were on the porch doing their school lessons.

The next morning we took a train to Pasuruan, which was a sleepy and oppressively hot town right at sea level. It seemed canals were the major features in the hot and barren town. There was the usual pasar, *aloon-aloon*, and a Mohammed missegit, and some very fine Chinese and Dutch residences. We stayed two nights at Hotel Insulinde, a most beautiful Chinese hotel. For the tropics it was cool, comfortable and clean, with colored tile baths and a cleanly swept patio with trees and ferns.

We made arrangements with a taxi driver for early morning. At five thirty A.M. we started out for the Tosari and Bromo volcanoes. We were well on the way by sunrise, and gradually ascended to the first mountain village of Pasrepan. The morning air was bracing and as we drove higher the air became cool and fine. The road rose steeply to the next village, which was Poespo. As we passed private Dutch mansions on the way. We also caught views of the valley below and the sea toward Saura Baya. The winding road rose past rocky cliffs and ravines smothered in tropical vegetation and luxuriant foliage. We enjoyed excellent scenery the whole route. We saw many native women and men walking, balancing huge loads on their heads. All of them carried umbrellas, since it rained every day. Large carts, pulled by slow-moving oxen, blocked our way many times, but it was a delightful drive of forty kilometers in the Tinnger Mountains to the highest mountain resort approximately 6,000 feet. The climate was ideal — much like that of England in June. It was an enchanting spot after the hot tropical lowlands. The village was perched on a rocky crag, like an eagle's nest, and commanded a superb view of the valley, mountains, and sea extending to Sura Baya and the island of Madura.

There was a huge ravine at the foot of Tosari, and both sides of the mountain slopes were cultivated from valley to peak, which reminded us of Switzerland and its mountain terrain. No incline seemed too steep to be cultivated, and all the land was remarkably terraced. It grew many varieties of vegetables, especially corn. The finest corn of Java was grown there.

The village had several good hotels and many little bungalows to rent. One hotel, called Bromo, was high above the village on a most beautiful spot with a splendid view. Here, temperate flowers like hydrangeas and roses bloomed along side fine cabbages, peaches and plums.

By foot, we started to climb Bromo volcano at seven thirty A.M. Tosari seemed spoiled to us with too much tourist atmosphere. But, we were a part of that package too. The trail wound gradually upward through beautiful forests of pines and giant tree ferns. Our trail headed downhill for about a mile and then, once more, began to climb. The clouds surrounded us as we began. The air was excellent. We carried wraps, a small lunch, water bottles, and an umbrella. We picked wild nasturtiums along the trail. Lantana grew wild everywhere. There were white, bell-shaped flowers on large bushes, dripping with misty dew. On the way, we met two Chinese men being carried down in sedan chairs, with eight Javanese coolies to each chair. The sight disgusted us, for it seemed the coolies were asked to do inhuman labor, and the uneven trail was slippery and steep.

We reached the rim of the crater at eleven A.M. and saw that it was still an active volcano. At the summit of the last steep climb we had a panoramic view of the great flat sand-sea below. The smoking Bromo, and one other perfectly coned crater, rose from the black-barren sand. We stood 1,000 feet above the sand-sea which was a great oval about five miles long and three miles wide and shut in by high mountains. Nothing but a few tufts of grass grew out of the black surface. Big white clouds of sulfur belched from Bromo, and we could smell the fumes even as far away as we were. To reach the crater we had to descend into this sand-sea, cross it, almost circle the middle cone peak at the base, and climb concrete steps up the lava slopes to the rim. We began this descent and met an English woman returning, being carried in a sedan chair by eight coolies.

We bought a fresh cabbage from a mountain native, guiding a ladened pony. Then we started climbing over the hardest and toughest piece of downward climbing we had ever experienced. The trail was full of great boulders and ruts and was very slippery wet, and torturously steep. Joe, with his rubber-soled shoes, had to be very careful. Our knees trembled with fatigue. Below, the sand sea looked like a mass of shallow rivers and water waves, but we discovered it was perfectly dry. The effect was an optical illusion produced by the wind blowing the sand. In about twenty minutes we descended 1,000 feet. Then we began a long trek across the flat, black-sand sea. It was utterly deserted, except for three ragged wild-looking natives whom we passed. On the mountain slopes surrounding the sand sea were cultivated fields, but nothing was cultivated on the sand and cinders.

We half-circled the extinct cone alongside Bromo. We saw ugly black and white lava slopes. There was no cone or symmetrical peak, but just a rough, forbidding and barren erupted piece of mountain. We climbed down its slope. Suddenly a driving rain came, chilling us to the bone, and we wrapped our coats about us. The sulfur became choking. We descended until we reached the concrete staircase rising almost perpendicularly. Our feet had almost given out by the time we got to the rim. But the stupendous sight made us forget our fatigue. We stood there on the narrow rim looking down over five hundred feet into a gigantic rugged hole, from the bottom of which furious clouds of steam and sulfur rose. There were moments when we could make out a boiling, hissing mass of yellow and green molten lava below. We dared not move about on the rim for it was dangerously slippery and narrow. On one side was the yawning crater; and on the other side, the rough outer lava slopes. The temperature changed in a moment from great heat to almost freezing. In spots on the rim we had to move about on our hands and knees as it was too slippery to trust our feet.

It was one of the most impressive sights we had ever seen. It took our breath away with wonder and surprise. We only remained on the rim about fifteen minutes, as the sulfur fumes burnt our eyes and choked us. We descended to a safer slope, beyond the steps and the fumes, where we sat to eat our lunch. The slopes of the crater were covered with cooled lava, and the ground beneath was warm and sounded hollow to each foot tread. It was awe-inspiring to sit thus on smoking ground, but we were uneasy about a possible eruption. The sun came out while we ate; and in a few minutes we all received a sunburn that would have taken all day in the California sun. We started our return trek over the grueling upward grade above the sand-sea, and on through the wooded mountain trail. It rained now and then making the hike cool and pleasant.

In three hours we were again in Tosari feeling we had enjoyed a most wonderful day. Nearing Tosari, we picked raw carrots from the cultivated fields. A native on horseback came along and stopped. I thought he was a constable or something as he waited and waited. Suddenly, I realized he wished to cross the small bridge on which Kane was sitting changing his socks. We called to Kane to move over, and the native, with a thankful smile, nodded and crossed.

In Tosari, we went to a native restaurant for hot tea and fruit while our taxi driver waited. His taxi was loaded with fresh fruit and cabbages from the highlands for his family. We arrived safely at the hotel where we bathed and rested. The next morning, we took an early train to Banyuwangi.

The train ride between Rambipudji and Banyuwangi afforded beautiful scenery. We saw mountain ranges from both sides of the railroad track as it ran through rolling hills of rubber plantations, coffee, kapok, rice paddies, and copra farms. Coffee trees were shaded by taller trees. Again, it was just a riot of tropical splendor, deep cliffs, rivers and waterfalls. This scenery was a relief after flat sugar cane and tobacco fields around Pasuruan. We saw large troops of wild monkeys from our train window. The mountain streams were the clearest and cleanest that we had seen in this section of Java. A heavy rain storm had come before we arrived in Banyuwangi. We had descended to sea level and were again in warm-sticky air.

Banyuwangi, (meaning sweet water) was in a low area. Three years previously, it had been plagued with malaria, typhoid, and dysentery, but the Dutch government had corrected the situation. There were three doctors working on isolating various varieties of malaria mosquitoes. There were terrible, filthy swamps along the beach where natives lived. The natives in the kampongs, along the railroad, were browner and wilder looking than those in West Java.

We found picturesque fishing villages with narrow, crooked streets. A river ran through a village overgrown with tropical jungle. Animal life was quite abundant here. Wild monkeys, antelope, and tigers lived in virgin forests about fifteen miles away. Recently, two antelope ran into the schoolyard and were captured. Wild monkeys were a real menace to the crops.

This part of Java was the richest agriculturally since it produced fine coffee and rubber. It also supplied all of Java with rice. All the fishermen had sailing boats and outrigger canoes. They were said to be able fishermen and seamen.

The Banyuwangi natives were known for their honesty and would return anything they found. Often they would for weeks seek for the owner. But this reputation was being spoiled now by some "bad elements" coming in from central Java.

We stayed in a Chinese hotel, Niesaue. The Chinese hotels here were exceptionally clean and orderly. We made some purchases in a Japanese department store and learned that the Japanese were introducing chain department stores all over the Indies competing with small Chinese and native stores. They were clever people. The Japanese we met seemed lonesome for their homeland. One Japanese boy in the store asked too high a price for some canteens we wanted. We made him an offer, but he refused. We told him we had been to his country and talked about some cities that he knew. He was so glad to know we had been in his country and liked it, that he reduced his price to our offered bargaining price.

We met Mr. Reynders, a student of philosophy, who had lived in Java twenty years or more. He was interested in Javanese folklore and customs, and told us many things about them. He enjoyed the old Javanese legends immensely. After being in the Dutch East Indies so long, he still found the natives most interesting, and he claimed their language was quite symbolic. I personally believe he exaggerated, as we did not find much depth to the Javanese culture.

*****

The Javanese are superstitious but not fanatical in their religions. Their Mohammedism is different from that of the Arabs. It is mixed with Javanism and old Hinduism. This is true especially in Central Java. They leave other religions and beliefs alone and are tolerant but wish to be left alone to their beliefs. They are a very happy and quiet people as long as they have their little rice, fish and tobacco. But, Dutch rule is impoverishing them and yet making them want more and more than ever before. The mind of the Javanese is simple - not as complicated as that of the Chinese and Japanese. The Javanese eat no dogs and are much afraid of them. There is some superstition connected with it. Very few dogs are to be seen. They eat no pigs. They love birds.

*****

Mr. Reynders gave us some interesting information during the few hours we spent with him. He believed the Dutch government could serve as a model for colonization; for the people are contented, and there are only 15,000 soldiers in all the islands.

There were very few foreigners in Banyuwangi. As we passed down the streets in our shorts, khaki shirts, and tropical hats, all natives seem to wonder where we were from and where we were going. All sorts of stories were whispered about us.

Hadji Tabrani, the King of the out-riggers in Banyuwangi, walked us through the street. We wanted to hire his Sri-Bali outrigger to go over to Bali on January 22, 1932. Since everybody in the village knew him, they kept asking him in Malay where he would take us, and he in turn answered, "To Tjupel." Their second question was whether we were English.

On our way, still looking for oarsmen to take us to Bali in a native craft, we came upon several Javanese women. They had delicate faces as well as well-built graceful figures and were eager to assist us in finding the seamen. By now, we were masters of a limited Malay vocabulary, but unfortunately the language changed as we advanced towards Eastern Java. We found we had to start all over again. Because the heat was so terrific, we were forced to take pony carts instead of walking. It was surprising how fast those little animals could move in such a hot climate. It must be in their breed.

While strolling along the beach, we found there was nothing but muck and filth, and this was too much for our noses. The natives were clean but had no idea about sanitation and the sources of tropical fevers. This is one area where government effort could make an impact by cleaning up this source of disease.

At ten P.M., we climbed into Mr. Hadji Tabrani's pride and joy, the Sri Bali. Other outriggers, slightly smaller, surrounded us. For half and hour there was much talk between the natives on the pier, questioning where we were going and peering down at the boat. Then all was quiet until we left with the tide at eleven P.M. The sound of gamalin music floated over the water. We could see tall masts of other sailing vessels visible in the bright moonlight. We could clearly see the three volcanic peaks behind Banyuwangi. A few natives got into other outriggers.

We had the Sri Bali to ourselves; it regularly carried fifteen passengers and two oarsmen. Hadji Tabrani came to see if we were comfortably settled. A canvas was spread over the deck, and a roll of straw placed under the canvas for a pillow. Two Javanese seamen came aboard, took off their hats and coats, and put them in a tin box. Each took an oar at each end of the craft, and we set sail. Four other outriggers sailed out of the harbor with us. The sail was hoisted before we were out of the harbor. It caught the breeze, and we glided smoothly out to sea under a brilliant full moon. The tall palms were silhouetted against the light sky. A more perfect setting we could not imagine.

The Sri Bali was six feet wide amid ship, and about twenty-five feet long from bow to stern. The main canoe was about two feet wide and a deck was built on top of it. It was the most perfect South Sea voyage I could ever have dreamed. Of all my sea travels, I had never had a more enjoyable voyage than this. The full-blown sails of the five outriggers on that moonlit water, with volcanoes and palms in the background, was a most lovely sight. For the first part of the voyage, we had no covering over our heads except the stars. The oarsmen from the different outriggers called to one another. These outriggers were remarkably seaworthy. Pitching and rolling was checked by the outriggers on each side of the craft making the voyage physically and spiritually enjoyable.

Kane and Lee were full of commonplace remarks, as usual, and perpetually eating. But Joe and I did not mind, as we had come to accept stoically their company.

We laid on our backs and watched the moon, the stars, the stray clouds, and the sail. The boatmen sat cross-legged and rested their tired arms as the wind carried us along. The oarsman in the stern rowed some and handled the rudder while the oarsman in the bow rowed some and handled the sail as we skimmed along.

After an hour or two, rain clouds blotted out the moon and drops began to fall. Skillfully and quickly, palm thatched mats were placed above us on the bamboo frame, which formed a roof-support. We used a sweater and an overcoat to protect ourselves from the stray drops blowing in. The boatmen, not minding the rain, remained outside the roof on the bow and stern. As the sky cleared, we could see the moon appear, as well as the receding coast of Java with its volcanoes. We were nearing the coast of Bali. It had been a perfect romantic and ideal South Sea Island sail. We dozed and awoke many times entranced by the marvelous night. The ever-changing clouds occasionally covered the mountain peaks.

About four-thirty A. M., we awoke from our naps to heavy raindrops and the scraping of more roof matting being placed above us. The crew shouted crisp orders to one another. The rain came down harder, and the roof was lowered so we couldn't see outside anymore. Wind blew, and the craft bounced and shivered. Curt words exchanged by our seamen resulted in the sail coming down with a bang and being secured. The seamen had shed nearly all their clothes, and the rain streamed down their bodies. We crouched under the shelter that had begun to leak a tiny bit, here and there. The rain was so dense; we couldn't see the other canoes or land. The boatmen called into the darkness to the other boats, but there was too much noise from the rain and wind for the others to hear. Suddenly, our anchor was dropped, oars fastened, and we heard hurried conversation between the two men as they pointed their fingers out to sea; and so, our craft was made ready for a squall.

Shivering and chattering, the Javanese crawled into the sheltered deck, holding their sides, to keep warm. The wind was chilly, and they were drenched. They lit cigarettes and squatted placidly awaiting the end of the little storm. We looked at the watch and when we told them it was five A.M, they pointed to the dim shore and said "Tjupel". We knew we were at our destination, and only awaiting daylight to land, instead of being miles from land in a squall. Thus we waited a gray daylight.

Here, the outrigger proved her stability and seaworthiness. The outriggers to each side served as balancers and shock absorbers for every pitch or roll. No heavy sea could overturn such a craft unless one of its outriggers snapped off.

A solitary lighthouse blinked evenly. As daylight came, the boatmen put on dry shirts and cotton trousers and began to pull up anchor and row toward shore. We sailed in until the keel scraped the sand. A stake was driven into the sand with a heavy rope attached to the canoe. The other outriggers did the same until a whole row of them lined the breaker's edge. Many craft set out for Banjoewangi as we came in.

Tjupel, Bali

The light disclosed a typical beach scene of blackish sand, with tall coconut palms up to the sand line, and one or two little palm-and-bamboo huts. Six or seven men and boys ran to the arriving outriggers holding their sarongs up about their waists as they waded in the water. All were friendly and curious when they saw white passengers, and some came out and onto the craft for awhile. The rain began again, and the incoming tide dashed the boat about. Always thinking of the craft first, the boatmen peeled off their shirts and outer trousers, and jumped into the surf, took off the anchor, and waded out with it to make it secure a little distance from the beach. The craft was now safe. We waited about half and hour for the rain to abate. We took off our shoes and socks, and Joe, his shorts. The local boys waded out and carried our packs to shore. Joe jumped in and waded to the beach, while our captain carried me to the sandy beach. We all ran barefooted across the beach to a little bamboo-and-palm hut that served as a native dwelling and restaurant. Chickens, cats, goats, dogs and monkeys ran about. The only woman there was the cook. The whole tiny village of about fifteen men and boys came to the grass hut to see us. With our few words of Malay and sign language, we talked and laughed for half an hour. They served us black coffee, thick as mud. An older man killed a chicken for us to eat while we were there. How kind and good-natured they were! So hospitable, even though they had nothing to gain from us. We washed our feet from a well in a field nearby. Alongside, was a bamboo platform with a palm roof wherein stood a Malay at prayer. He bowed low like the Mohammedans do.

Three one-horse carriages stood by waiting to take us to Negara. We wanted to hike the seven kilometers, but the rain had made the roads too muddy. So we bargained, agreed on a fare, piled into two carriages, and left our waving group of new friends. It poured rain all the way but we fared rather well, receiving just a little soaking.

The road passed many isolated huts, here and there, amidst planted coconut groves. Huge piles of coconuts used for copra were in many yards. We noticed the style of native huts had changed. We were in Bali! A different atmosphere prevailed which was hard to describe. Stately Balinese women, bare from the waist up, passed us on the road balancing great baskets of produce on their heads. Natives plowed and hoed in the rice paddies even as it rained. No one seemed to mind the rain at all. We passed our first Balinese Hindu temple. There was something compact and beautiful about it.

Negara, Bali

We arrived at the village of Negara in the driving rain, and unloaded our packs at the Dutch *pasangrahan* which housed three Dutch officials. It was much different from Java. We thought descriptions of Bali had been exaggerated from all we had read, but just this tiny village had proved Bali to be unspoiled. There were naked women walking around with large baskets on their heads, and in the stream alongside the road, they sat and bathed. Their faces and figures were strikingly beautiful. They wore their hair loose, brought to the top of their heads on one side, and then allowed to fall gracefully. The small children were lovely. Many of the little girls had curly black hair and looked like little gypsies. They wore no clothing but silver anklets, and bracelets. They often wore a little metal disk in front, like a fig leaf, fastened by a narrow string around their waists. Betel nut was chewed here, too, but mostly by the older women. We saw mean-looking, miserable dogs in every compound, and we learned that the Balinese kept pigs. Both of these things, we did not see in Java.

The native huts, made of woven and split bamboo with palm-thatched roofs, were always in large clusters, or compounds, with sheds for the animals. These sheds had tall, steep roofs. Within the eaves, fodder and grain was kept for the horses and pigs which were tied below. Other raised tall-roofed sheds were granaries for the family's rice and corn. A three-foot adobe brick wall, painted with whitewash, was built around each compound to prevent erosion from the heavy rains. The top of the wall, all around, had a grass-thatched roof of dry palm leaves placed to look like a slanting roof. These roofs peaked at the top and slopped down each side, and gave a distinct look to each group of huts.

Within the compound walls, were from two to six little shrines raised on four-or five-foot posts along with small thatched huts. Even though each roof was finished differently, one usually had a round knob and another a tall peaked roof. This was probably symbolic of something. We made the acquaintance of a young boy from Sumatra who spoke good Dutch, and was stranded in Bali without a job. He pointed out to us the neatly arranged groups of offerings on the ground before many gateways to the compounds. There would be bits of rice, tobacco, betel nut, flower petals, and smoldering coconut husks, sending forth smoke. These were forms of offerings to the Hindu gods. When the offerings were too numerous, they were taken down and put on the ground at the entrance. The offerings were always on banana leaves.

*****

The Balinese Hindu Temples are groups of altars and grass pagoda-like structures, all out in the open, surrounded by a wall and one large altar predominating. Hindu ornaments adorn the entrance gate at the wall. They are indeed a pleasing and artistic arrangement.

*****

Never had we come across such kind and lovable people. There was always a smile, a greeting, or a word of gratitude on their lips. When we ventured into a private yard, the owner often came out smiling graciously, and showed us the things in which we seemed interested and tried to explain the customs and showed us the finest courtesy.

The usual small, native pasar was filled with women vendors. Many of them wore fresh flowers in their hair as is Polynesian custom. Small shops lined one street. The natives looked at us kindly, and were not surprised or afraid.

We met Fan Bulow, the assistant resident of several provinces of Bali, and he told us many interesting things. He had lived five years in Negara and had built the roads and steel and stone bridges in Southwest Bali. He also had full judicial power. Negara was the main village and capital of Djembrana province which was the richest agriculturally.

The Balinese used to send their undesirables to Djembrana province since it was an inaccessible section.

When the Chinese came to Bali, they brought Chinese money with them which is still used today in daily trading. These brass and bronze pieces have a hole in the middle.

Many Germans and Swiss were in Bali as plantation owners. Bulow found the caste system here very interesting. Even the higher society women came to him with undressed upper body, but should a stranger come to their houses, the first thing they would do would be to cover themselves. Jackets did not mean high caste, as prostitutes wore jackets.

Bulow knew of no European who knew the Balinese language for it was one of the hardest to learn. He told of a man who for ten years had tried to compile the first Balinese dictionary, and only got to the letter "F".

The Balinese tell interesting stories. They claimed that every five years there came great cloudbursts which cause rivers to overflow and sweep away bridges. Mr. Bulow believed this to be true. They also claimed that every five years, there would be an exceptionally good coconut crop.

There was one avenue in Negara on which two rows of trees were loaded with white and yellow cranes. The trees were so full of cranes that every time we passed through, we had to open the umbrella for protection against the droppings.

From Negara, we went by bus to the outpost Pulukan, or as far as the bus could go with the bridges being washed out. The village consisted of only a few straw huts along the riverbank. Men were constructing a temporary bridge, and chopping away the tremendous tree which had dammed up the water. Only one foreigner lived in this spot. He was a German who owned a large copra plantation.

A recent cloudburst and a hurricane had washed away many bridges on the southwestern shore road. On the opposite side of the river, we caught a bus which went as far as the next washed-out bridge at the Selabi River. The view was beautiful as we rode along the thundering surf and the black rock beach where the jungle grew right to the water's edge. There seemed to be an endless number of rivers that washed to the sea from the near-by mountains, and these tumbling rivers offered exciting scenery.

It was January 24, 1932. We found it was hard to believe the distance we had come and the wonderful experiences we had since August 19, 1931.

At the Selabi River, half-naked natives greeted us from the opposite bank, but there was not even a sampan to get us across. So, the boys removed their shorts, socks and shoes, and carried their packs high, and waded across the swift river. TThe water is some spots came up to their waistlines. A jolly and sturdy barefooted native took me onto his back, and thus we crossed. Then we put our clothes on and started to hike. It was some seven or eight kilometers to the next river. No buses were running at all. The scenery was marvelous. One moment we were near the rough, pounding surf, and the next moment we were on a knoll, or on a small bridge looking down on the muddy river tumbling beneath us among the thick vegetation. We saw many gray and black wild monkeys jumping in the trees, on the ground, and drinking from the river. Another traveler, who had forded the river before us, was walking ahead. We met him at a roadside shelter just as he was preparing to leave, but he put down his pack and sat with us. We had a fine, large papaya with us so we cut it open and offered him a piece. He refused, saying he was Mohammedan and this being a holy month, he could not eat or drink between noon and six P. M. He would not leave ahead of us, but took his pack and started after we had started — perhaps out of respect or out of a need to be alone.

Needless to say, it was hot in the sun, and we perspired! In fact, Joe's back and pack dripped with sweat. Finally, after passing over several more rivers, we came to Tukatbalian River. There was a sight! The largest river of Bali was in a mad torrent, and a large, concrete-steel bridge was completely gone. It had been carried a few hundred yards down toward the roaring sea. On the road just above the river, and stuck for many days, were five trucks lined up and filled with Herr Bulow's furniture bound for Singaradja. An improvised outrigger canoe, held by a wire cable which spanned the river, was pulled across.

This was the only means of crossing. The ferryman spoke some Dutch and told us there was no village here, or anywhere further on, where we could stay. He kindly offered us an improvised shelter which had been constructed for the truck drivers. It was a clean, newly-made, bamboo and palm hut with one large and two smaller partitions. Down river, along the banks, was another new community dwelling for the men who were working on the bridge. The ferryman gave instructions to a Malayan boy, and our quarters were hastily made comfortable. We took towel and soap, and a pair of bathing shorts for Joe, and went to the river to bathe. The boys undressed and sat in the water scrubbing. I, in brassier and tucked up skirt, also soaped and washed. Natives all about us were semi-nude, bathing and playing. When we came back from bathing, we found a palm partition along one side of our room and soft, and fresh palm branches on the floor with clean mats on top, and with a mattress and two pillows brought from somewhere. Nails were pounded into the bamboo supports from which we could hang our hats, cameras and baskets, and a nail to hang a small kerosene lamp. In the middle of the shelter was a table covered with a cloth, and four chairs around it. Five women in sarongs offered us fruit. We felt fine after washing up. The day had been hot and we had walked a great deal. Three pots of tea were brought to us with cups, saucers and sugar. We dined with the scant provisions we brought with us from Negara, — bread, eggs, and peanuts. On the table was a large bunch of bananas for us. I put up mosquito netting, and we retired early. The full moon reflecting on the river was an exquisite sight.

The boys and the women sang far into the night. We woke up a few times and heard them still singing. Their melodies were lively ones as well as melancholy. It reminded us of some old Jewish melodies with Allah mentioned often. We had no mosquitoes but quite a few ants, and the palm branch ribs were a bit bumpy. Just the same, it was beautiful sleeping thus, in the semi-open alongside a great river in Bali, under a full moon.

After we were in bed, the ferryman brought in a pot of boiled chicken and soup. We didn't know how to thank him, but asked him to bring the warmed soup to us in the morning. Moonlight shown in on us between stray rain clouds.

We awoke on the morning of the 25th, at about four-thirty. By five, they brought us hot tea, and a pan with twenty-one boiled eggs, along with the hot chicken soup. It was delicious. Balinese hospitality! We tried to give some money to the young boy who served us, but he wouldn't take it.

We went to the river to wash, and Joe shaved. At seven A. M. we took our leave and crossed over the river in the frail outrigger, which had been fastened by rope to the stretched cable. I insisted that the ferryman take money for his kindness and hospitality, and he finally accepted. He bade us good-bye as we started on a long trek of eight kilometers to Antasari

The roadway wound up, down and around beautifully terraced fields. As we climbed higher, we had a panoramic view of the sea and the island of Java. Natives, going to work in the fields, formed a long procession and some women came along carrying loads on their heads. We crossed more rivers and then turned inland. We stopped beside a rice canal and bathed our arms and faces. The sun was hot already so early in the day.

Antasari

At Antasari, we walked almost through the village before we knew we were in it. A roadside mileage sign was the only thing that told us the crossroads met here. We walked along the roadway and saw huts and walls on either side. We put our knapsacks on the bench of a small roadside stand that sold a few meager things, and inquired about a bus to the next town but couldn't make ourselves understood since the Balinese didn't seem to know much Malay. The natives crowded around us astonished to see whites. Those passing on the road stopped and looked, and one went and called another. Older children and mothers brought their babies to see us. Many tried to speak to us. They noticed my blond hair and the beads around my neck. We heard the word *blanda*, "white," used often. On the counter were some cookies, cut potatoes, some shredded tobacco, rolled betel leaf, and a tray of banana patties with some shredded coconut. The Balinese picked pieces of potato, or banana, tossed down Chinese coppers, one for each piece. I gave some pomelo to one baby and he liked it. One little boy knew a little Dutch, but not enough for us to understand him. We could find but one bus that ran to the next village, so we decided to take a stroll.

We followed a group of beckoning, laughing boys into a kampong and entered a one-room hut raised above the ground. Within, was a great array of gamelan gongs and instruments, bronze gongs and drums made of wood and hide. These boys, straight away squatted each beside his instrument, and played music for us. Some of the instruments, such as hollowed pots of brass and bronze pieces, were hit with metal hammers. Others were tapped in a rhythmic tattoo with bamboo sticks, They finished one piece and had just begun another as a bus arrived. We hailed it and found it crowded. Opposite us sat a handsome, aristocratic youth with a briefcase. He seemed reserved, yet he spoke Dutch and asked many questions. His fine bearing and beautiful face shone like a light in the bus. We felt a connection between us. He showed pronounced courtesy as he held my basket and always kept rearranging our things each time they were moved to let a passenger get off. The bus went no further than the village of Butangsel.

Butangsel

We didn't think this was a lovely place, as it was devoid of trees. Walls and huts were ill-kept, and there were countless miserable dogs howling and barking at our heels. We asked about the temple we saw a few yards ahead, and the Balinese boy immediately took us there. The temple was no longer used. There were ferns growing beautifully out of thatched altar roofs, and moss colored the old red bricks. There was not much inside except empty altars, but the entrance gate, pillars, and images were well preserved, as well as the old gold leaf on the carved steps where grotesque faces and animal figures were carved. All Balinese temples, of any size, use red brick trimmed with white as the building material . This temple of Butangsel was centuries old, from Hindu times. We then took the road towards Pudjungan accompanied by our Balinese friend.

Ida Bagoes Moedra was one of those souls scattered over the earth that thinks for himself, but has found none in Bali whom he could divulge his thoughts. We liked him from the first moment. His face expressed his character and spoke to us a language which we readily understood and appreciated, but seldom found.

Moedra took to us immediately, and we felt as if we had known each other for years. He told us many interesting facts about the caste system in Bali. He belonged to one of the highest Brahmin families in Bali. His father, who lived in Singaradja, had nine sons of which Moedra is the eldest. Moedra was twenty-two years old, but we thought of him as much older, for he was quite mature. The discipline in a Balinese family was severe and put great responsibility on the eldest son. Moedra worked with the Dutch residents in public offices for a number of years. Then he became a controller of finances for the Bali Volks Bank, a post that his father wanted him to take against Meodra's wishes. He had no say-so about his own life. He had married one year previously because his father wanted it. He knew his wife only six months before marriage. He had stolen in the night to see his future wife, which was strongly condemned by Brahmans. If he had been discovered, Moedra would have been killed by his father. He had to take his father's orders, and he had to marry because his father wanted him to feel more responsibility. Inwardly he rebelled, but his kind nature made it possible for him to carry on.

We took a long walk with him through kampongs and strange courtyards. We found people pounding rice, cutting wood and doing other domestic chores. He went to see five different people and introduced us to all of them, and also did the talking for us since none of them knew a word of Dutch.

The power of the Brahmins over the people used to be unlimited. The people were their virtual slaves. Their power lessened considerably after the Dutch came, but it was still very strong. Moedra had progressive ideas but would never think of exercising his powers. He knew well the teachings and philosophy of Gandhi, Tagore, and Nehru, To demonstrate his Brahman power to us, he asked a Balinese maiden who passed on the road, carrying a heavy basket of fruits on her head, to go down on her knees. He just gave her a sign with his hand, and she did so instantly. He took two little bunches of a tropical palm fruit and told her to rise. She then continued on her way. Although he did not often exercise his powers, the natives feared and respected him. Large groups of people crowded around us as soon as we stopped in any one place, but dispersed as soon as someone noticed Moedra coming.

Moedra neglected work one day and gave us all of his time. He treated us as if we were old friends. He said many times, he felt like a brother to Joe. I told him that perhaps we had been brothers in a previous life.

He settled us in a little house and ordered a vegetarian meal for us to be cooked by a native woman. He offered to pay the taxi man the next morning but I would not let him. He offered a mirror to Tonia, and brought her roses and some fruits in a bottle.

Around six o'clock in the evening, after we were through writing our notes and Moedra had finished with his accounting, he asked us to go with him to a private house and hear native music, a flute and drum orchestra. Eventually, the whole village followed us to the music performance and the room was filled. The flute was sweet and the drums were sonorous.

After this intimate evening, we returned to our little house to sit down to our simple meal. Moedra insisted that we three should eat together first, and Lee and Kane would eat by themselves afterwards. This could have been an unpleasant situation. He could not stand their presence. It was a cozy room, and the meal was one of the most pleasant ones we had had for a long time. He spoke very little, his face told many tales.

Unexpectedly, a group of elderly men came to see Moedra to give an explanation as to why they could not pay their debts. This prolonged the evening until nine o'clock, but we enjoyed every moment of it. The old weather-beaten men did much talking. Some of them had their mouths filled with tobacco for the usual betel cleaning. They presented an interesting study to us. Moedra took their signatures by thumb printing the right and left thumbs. After completing their business, they asked questions about us.

Moedra, with whom we had lived for some time, asked the supervisor of the gamelan organization of the district to prepare a special concert and dancing in the public feast square. The concert and dancers patiently waited for us as we had a long walk along a bumpy and winding path, by flashlight, to get to the public square.

On that evening, all the villagers assembled around the open temple. One little kerosene lamp, suspended by a wire, gave some light to the yard, casting weird shadows about. On one side of the open square, the musicians sat on mats with their instruments grouped in front of them. Workers in their rice fields by day, these men and boys became accomplished musicians at night. News of the unexpected performance spread, and a steady stream of villagers came with offerings of fragrant flowers, incense and little banana-leaf plates of cooked rice for the poora gods.

During the first half-hour, the gamelan played a beautiful group of compositions. Then there emerged, from one side, a most fantastic figure: a large animal, some eight feet long, made of tooled and painted leather with long hair and a lion's head. Two boys were beneath it, one in the front and the other in back. We could see only their legs. The beast went first to the poora where the village priest consecrated it by filling the air with incense, since every Balinese dance has some religious significance. Then the music, called the Lion Dance, began and the beast slowly swayed into the rhythms of a dance to ward off evil spirits. The head was moveable as were the jaws. The figure plunged forward, reared backwards, turned its head and gnashed its teeth in a most realistic fashion. The two boys beneath the skin danced in complete co-ordination, making the manipulation of that huge figure a splendid piece of pantomime. The music grew faster, and the dance became more animated. It finally ended, after almost an hour, in a wild climax with the beast triumphant over the invisible demons. The most remarkable thing about the performance was the perfect harmony between the two dancers beneath the huge animal skin and the orchestra. In the same quiet manner with which they had gathered, the villagers silently dispersed and disappeared into the darkness after the performance.

The little island of Bali rings with music from one end to the other. Music is as much a part of Bali as the mountains and rivers. At no time could we lose that Balinese symphony of tones. Late at night, out of the darkness, we heard the deep, vibrant bronze-gongs ringing for hours. And during the day, music drowned out all other sounds in every village. Besides being a complete orchestra unto itself, no Balinese festivity is given without the gamelan: "the music of the island."

We first heard gamelan music in Java. There, it was beautiful, but in a melancholy, monotonous way. It could be heard only in certain parts of Java, like in Djokja Karta and Solo, where the last remnants of Javanese culture could be found carefully cultivated within the walled-in courts of the Sultans.

*****

Gamelan Orchestra

The gamelan orchestra consists of six types of instruments. There are those similar to small, low xylophones with wooden bars, and those with curved bronze bars, which are tapped with small hammers and padded sticks. Another instrument is a long, low row of graduated pot lids of brass, with hollow knobs in the center, fitted loosely over hollow brass bowls set in a wooden frame. These are tapped with bamboo sticks as the musicians sit cross-legged on the ground. Bronze gongs of various sizes and magnificent tones are an important part of a Balinese orchestra. The gongs swing from wooden frames and are played with padded drumsticks. Brass cymbals and drums complete the ensemble. There are twenty-eight musicians in all. The drums are fashioned with rawhide stretched over light split bamboo frames. They are long and slightly narrow at each end and are played by holding them, lightly, on one knee. The drummers, like the rest, sit cross-legged on the ground, tapping both ends of the drum with dexterous hands and fingers. The tempo is always led by the two drummers, who are the most highly trained musicians of the group, since they know every other instrument perfectly. The orchestra usually forms an open, three-sided rectangle, in the center of which are enacted the folk plays and dances.

The tone value of the gamelan is different from those of Western musical instruments. Instead of the half tones of our scale, their keys skip in intervals, which always produce a minor harmony. There is no written music in Bali. The melodies are handed down from one player to another. Compositions are learned as the composer hums to the orchestra, emphasizing the rhythms with the drum.

*****

The gamelan orchestra is unique in the world of music. Night after night we listened to it and soon distinguished the rich variety of melodies its music had. Indeed, within its limitations, it was almost as full in tone as a Western symphony orchestra. Some compositions reminded us of Wagner with deep gong tones in the background, making a continuous leitmotif that recurred endlessly; and at the same time, tempering the swift staccato tones of the other instruments. The gamelan can produce the softest pianissimo and the most glorious tone vibrations of the pulsing forte. We were more conscious of rhythm than of melody and of the tones that would not be produced by any other than a gamelan instrument.

Bali's music was a blending of the most wonderful syncopation of rhythms tempered by the exquisite tones of solemn deep-bronze gongs. The gongs alone could bring one into a state of ecstasy. The mellowness of their tones went through us like draughts of wine, or like moonlight. It was music that sent us wandering up and down, out of the sheer pain of joy its tones produce. It was liquid and haunting like a flowing brook. The melodies sang and the tempo expanded until the music became a pulsing, vibration of rhythms, while the players, swaying their naked torsos, seemed to become music personified. Each time the orchestra finished and the musicians began carrying away their instruments, we remained still for a few minutes afterwards, like people who had lost a treasure but could not realize it.

A small reed flute was also played on the island. At night, we could hear the plaintive notes of one flute or a delicate melodious piping of several accompanied by muted drums. No matter where we wandered in Bali, the music warmed our hearts day and night. These lovable people always led us, first of all, to their open community entertainment square, and played their music for us, — certainly a most beautiful form of hospitality.

After the concert, we took a stroll in the moonlight. It was beautiful. We walked slowly, gazing into the moonlit river and over the terraces of rice. We sang joyously, as our hearts had not been so light in many a day. The contrast between Moedra's presence and that of Lee and Kane, which we had endured for many days, was great. A delightful peace came over us, and we had a great longing and love for the island of Bali. We didn't speak much, but felt a great depth of joy.

We started back, and as we neared the village, we heard music and singing. In the moonlight, this bare little village was transformed into a fairyland. In the open, under the roof of the community assembly hut, was a native folk play being spoken, sung and danced by the children. The principal players were in the center on the dirt floor. On mats, seated on four sides, were two rows of boys opposite each other and two rows of girls opposite each other. Young girls and children took the principal roles, dressed in rare gold and silver leaf-appliquéd Balinese weaves. They had mastery of the most intricate arm and finger movements, precise foot positions and accompanying head movements. The chorus of girls was in special costumes and headdresses. Their long, black hair was bedecked with fresh and fragrant flowers. A small gamelan orchestra accompanied the alternate speaking, singing, and dancing. Now and then the chorus sang, and it was a jolly lively interlude accompanied by unison hand clapping.

The village people were grouped about enjoying every moment of the play. It was given especially for themselves and their own enjoyment. A little platform outside the hut held offerings to the gods, and a few tidbit stands were about. There were many comical situations, and the villagers laughed and laughed. Most of them who watched were rice farmers, burnt black from the sun.

About twelve-thirty A.M., we left. Moedra procured a raincoat for us as it threatened to rain. Slowly, we walked back, silently drinking in the beauty of the night and each other's company. Since it had cleared again, we spread the raincoat and Moedra's sarong on the ground and lay down in the moonlight.

It was so beautiful. We wanted to say many things, but the difficulties of not knowing enough Dutch hindered us. However, our mutual silence spoke more. Moedra, lying on his back, was like a beautiful, unspoiled faun, a part of nature in his exquisite Bali. Back at the little cottage and to our room we found Lee and Kane asleep. Moedra took the raincoat, went to the porch, and sat in a chair to sleep. The boys had his bed. We insisted he sleep with us in the other bed. Finally he assented and seemed happy about it. He placed his unfolded batik cap over the lamp to shade it. He sat up later to write a letter to his father which he wanted us to take to him. He expressed his wish that we would stay with his father in Singaradja. Moedra told us that he disliked Lee and Kane very much and would not have spoken to them in Antasari when the bus stopped at their hailing if we had not come up. At two A.M. we finally went to sleep with the little kerosene lamp, covered with Moedra's cap, turned very low. Five A.M. saw us rubbing the sleep from our eyes even though we had hardly slept. We were refreshed, I think, due to a deep spiritual peace. In the darkness we washed and bathed in the yard. We dipped water from a rainwater barrel with a coconut dipper. Moedra filled our basket with bananas and poured our tea, ignoring Lee and Kane. His face showed his sorrow at parting from us. He came with us for almost a mile. We just begged him not to come further, as he just had to walk back again. His eyes filled, and with a lingering handclasp, he placed in our palm a carved horn and bone monogram that he carried on his watch chain. We waved to him until we were out of sight, heavy-hearted, yet happy to know it was our privilege to know such a rare, beautiful character. Here in Bali, we had found one of the rare universal souls of the world. Into the early day we went, our first destination being Pupuan, just two kilometers away.

There were no buses available anywhere on this stretch, so after purchasing some hard crackers, we went on. We hiked over a gravel mountain road. The lovely scenery was ever changing with slopes of rice terraces, mountains, groups of Balinese huts, tropic palms, and other trees. A sudden rainstorm made us seek shelter in a hut used by the rice farmers. Later, along the road, we had to scramble into another shelter. The morning was cloudy and rainy, and although we got wet, the walking was more pleasant, and we made better time than if we were hiking in the hot sun. Kilometer after kilometer we walked. This island was so intimate and small, that again and again we saw the sea on both sides . At last we found the crossroads we were seeking. The signposts pointing to Singaradja, back to Tabanau, and one said Binnenweg, pointing towards a small mountain village.

There was no sign to Munduk, the place we wanted. This village was Subuk, where a twelve kilometers trail began through the mountains.

Subuk

We inquired about the way to Munduk, and everyone pointed to the steep trail, although our map indicated that there was an auto road there. The trail was better and shorter, so that's the way we went. The road led up and down, past little thatched mud huts and some jungle. It rained now and then, and we found the trail slippery in spots. The sun came out, and we perspired so much that Joe removed his shirt and lay it on the rocks to dry. The rain had been pleasant, and it was much better walking than on the seething gravel roadway. High up on a mountain, we came to a peaceful temple grounds shaded by trees. Under the shelter, and on a moist bamboo platform, we stretched out and snatched a snooze for half an hour. Then we went further passing through isolated mountain villages. Horrible mongrel dogs heralded our coming. On arriving at Plapuan it seemed that hundreds of starved canines barked at us. As were very hot and tired, we drank many cups of koppie and ate bananas, throwing the skins to the pigs in the street. At this place, as usual, the whole village came squatted down and watched us. Some of them had never before seen a white person.

The trail began to lead down along the rim of rice paddies. We heard a river below and, as we came to it, found that we had to wade across, so off came the shoes and socks. It was rather difficult crossing because the water rushed over the rocks, and covered the footholds. I splashed my skirt, which that was refreshing. From there the trail went up again, past another kampong, and we found ourselves on a highway in the village of Tundu. Here, the trail met the auto road. A tremendous chorus of dogs again greeted us until the place echoed with their barks and howls.

As the road passed through Tundu, it was bordered with large trees which gave a solid shade. The brick and mud walls of the yards on each side of the road were in good repair, but behind the walls, the huts were shabby. Inquiries told us Munduk was five kilometers — then seven kilometers — then nine kilometers away — so we just kept on going, this time on the roadway in the direction of Munduk. We began to climb again. The sun came out, and we sat to rest near some huts. The villagers ran down from the hill, squatted, and talked to us, but in a few minutes, a wind sprang up. The people rose in a hurry, shouted to us, and pointed to the sky. They beckoned to us to run up the path to their huts. It was just in time too, for before we reached the shelters, the rain was upon us, and it poured! We all crowded into a small porch, put our packs on a table, and laughed.

They asked us if we wanted some durian fruit. They brought another umbrella, and we all ran across the yard to the community shelter where a woman sold fried bananas. The young ones squatted on a straw mat playing a gambling game with two white balls in a soup plate. The people bought fried bits with Chinese coins, and the boys gambled with the same kind of money.

A pile of durians and a great jackfruit were under the shelter. The woman, who was the vendor, cut the jackfruit and sold the pieces. They offered us fruit and fried but we refused. We asked them if they had hot tea. No tea or koppie! All they had in that kampong were durians, jackfruit, and fried tidbits of bananas.

Munduk

In half an hour the rain stopped. A mile or so further up the road, we came to a small stand where we had hot tea. Then it began to rain again. The smoke from the fire nearly blinded us. At a distance, on a slope, we saw a large group of buildings that looked like it might be a pasangrahan. We asked the woman vendor and she shook her head, saying, "five kilometers more." We couldn't believe our ears, but pushed on further. The rain stopped again, quickly, as it does in the tropics. The air now was fine and cool. We arrived at the buildings we had seen from a distance and found a school and a gasoline station in a native kampong. Some boys throwing, dippers of water over themselves, stopped and told us the village of Munduk and the pasangrahan was three-kilometers. They asked us if we wanted an auto, but we declined. These last three-kilometers seemed longer than any we had hiked that day. It really was almost four and a half-kilometers by the signposts. At each turn we gazed expectantly thinking now here is the *pasangrahan*. Up and up we went to the very top of a mountain and then along its rim where we found the village. The huts and yards ran down steeply on each side of the center road. There was a small pasar, many temples, and a few Chinese-owned houses. We rested awhile to cool off before going to the pasangrahan at the very end of the road. It was a small house set in a well-kept rose and flower garden. A front verandah overlooked the village and terraces of rice. There were more mountain ranges, the sea, and peaks of Java beyond. The back verandah overlooked a deep, bamboo-covered ravine. There were rice terraces on the upward slopes of the mountain above and native huts clinging to the steep cloud covered-mountain slopes. The panorama was magnificent. The air was like a cool balm.

This little pasangrahan, managed by a Javanese, had four rooms for guests, two beds in each room, a modern basin, and running water. There was a dining room and large front and back verandahs with tables and chairs. The baths were clean, and there was a pool filled with river water, continually running through it. The walls of the house and inner rooms were woven bamboo painted over with plaster. We were the only guests. The room rates were reasonable, but the meals were priced high. So, we provisioned ourselves from the village pasar. After a general washing of ourselves, our clothes, and a change into fresh clothing, we felt fine.

That afternoon it poured rain again. We found that it rained every afternoon there. Woolen blankets and no mosquito netting bespoke of the climate. It was the first time in the Dutch East Indies that I had shivered in the bath. Joe brought a canteen of hot tea and some rice, and we dined with the eggs and some bananas that we had. We wrote a few notes and went to sleep, delightfully tired. We slept like dead ones after hiking that day from six A.M. to four P.M. a distance of some thirty-one kilometers, or over nineteen miles. The clouds and rain had helped us we walked in the heat of the tropics.

Next morning (January 27, 1932), we awoke and marveled again at the exquisite scenery. We decided to remain a couple of days and just rest and loaf in the coolness. We walked to the pasar and made purchases. We filled our canteens with fresh tea, bought steamed brown rice and roasted peanuts, bananas, some biscuits, and some fresh eggs, which the tea vendor boiled for us as we waited. They all laughed and talked about us, and some old women asked us, "makan Europea," which probably meant they thought we did not get European meals at the pasangrahan. They couldn't understand "white" people buying food from them. The day was spent writing and resting and reading.

*****

On the Classic Balinese Dance

The Legong dance is the most popular throughout the island. To witness is to enjoy a most beautiful artistic and emotional experience. In this dance, the poetic culture of Bali is exquisitely and emotionally expressed, and their ancient religious legends are enacted. Usually, two very young girls perform it. Their lithe, slender bodies are wound in a long, tight swathing of brilliantly-colored prada (—woven silk appliqué, with designs in gold and silver leaf—) their arms encased in long tight sleeves, and the feet remain bare. On their heads, fantastic gold headdresses quiver with a hundred tiny golden points and flowers, and in their hands, they carry brilliant paper and silken fans.

The postures of this dance are short and stiff with slightly bent knees; the long train of the costume forms a graceful line with the figure. Very often another dancer appears as a guardian garooda god, with a hairy headdress, mask, and great wings. This figure sits while the dancers move about in pantomime, speaking to it. Their ability for pantomime is wonderful, the more so when one realizes that the face remains absolutely serene and passive, except for sidewise movements of the eyes. It was like a uniform, unchanging mask that never smiles, yet, the dance tells its story beautifully and easily, in spite of it. The hand positions of these young girls are simply impossible for untrained hands to accomplish. The arms bend outwardly as if they have no bones. The head and neck moves from side to side without any shoulder movements, producing a subtle and angular grace. The arms, fingers and hands move, while the body stays, more or less, in the same pose at various angles— that of a twisted torso with knees slightly bent and turned outward.

A delicate refinement runs throughout all of Bali's dances. Such a highly developed technique is rarely achieved by adult dancers in the West. On temple feast days, and in the folk plays, dancing expresses as much as the spoken word and song. There are decided Indian or Hindu characteristics about Balinese dancing. The dances interpret Hindu legends brought to this semi-Polynesian island by Hindu missionaries twenty centuries ago. The young dancers are trained from infancy, and between twelve and twenty years of age, they perform.

*****

Dogs on Bali:

A book might be written about the dogs of Bali. Every village has hordes of them, and they all growl and bark in an ear-splitting, horrible din when any stranger approaches. They come to the road, stand in the yard and at the gate, barking to heaven, making it almost impossible for one person to hear another. One always knew he was approaching a village by the distant barking and howling. And, they were the most miserable, woe-be-gone, mangy, hairless, starved-out lot of canines the Lord had ever born. Almost hairless, and not an ounce of flesh on their bones, they just appeared as shrunken skin marred by sores and scars. Nobody fed them, as the people had nothing to give or spare. So, the dogs had to shift for themselves, which made for a vicious rivalry among the canines. Most all of them had a scar, an ear bitten off, or just a piece of tail. They continually nipped at each other, glowered, and scowled with teeth barred and lips curled for a few moments, but then they turned and went away. The stronger ones bit the weaker and the latter yelped and ran. They existed on bits of durian peel, pineapple peelings, jackfruit, and lapped up stray rice grains clinging to banana leaf wrappers.

We once saw a dog steal a cake from a vendor in the market, but it was not beaten for it. No one molested or hurt the dogs in Bali. They just shooed them away, nothing more. If some tidbit was thrown to a group, a code of honor seemed to exist, and each one hastily grabbed a bit closest to him and backed away, letting the others get their share. No one fondled or played with the dogs in Bali. They were utterly left alone. The Balinese religion probably had something to do with their not doing away with emaciated animals they could not feed.

*****

Mountain Lakes near Munduk

The most beautiful hiking excursion in Bali was along the picturesque mountain lakes of Tamblingan, Buyan, and Beratan. We left the *pasangrahan* at daybreak and took a foot trail that was rather strenuous at first, owing to the steep and continuous ascent. The trail led through tall, dadap trees which shaded wild coffee trees that grew wild here and there. The coffee trees were tall-scraggly ones, unkempt and lean, but it made the mountain sides look natural and rugged. Trees of coffee plants continually obstructed the trail. As the result of the hurricane, huge forest giants lay uprooted over the road.

The air was cool and invigorating; the ground was moist and covered with leaf mold. We met a few half-naked native woodsmen carrying curved scythes and knives. They bowed to us as they passed. On top of the ridge, where the steep trail ended, we saw our first view of Tamblingan. We had climbed from 750 meters at Munduk to 1362 meters at the ridge. Below, unspoiled, unused, and untouched, was a virgin lake. Grasses grew to the edge of the water while trees covered the upward slopes. No one, except perhaps a few natives, went to its shore. To gaze at that lake was like seeing silence personified. The trail was fairly level from here, and from between the jungle openings, we could see the lake below. The trail was a narrow footpath almost overgrown with wet grass and thick jungle growing on both sides. We passed strange wild fruits, parasitic vines, and countless orchids. Big wild monkeys shook the trees. Trees and brush were so thick; natives had to chop through them to open a path. Then came the second lake close by the first one, divided by a ridge between. This was lake Buyan. The path on the ridge led past this lake, and then turned abruptly to the tiny village of Tojo Ketipat, which was comprised of just three dilapidated shacks. As usual, a skinny little dog greeted us. The path widened becoming more of a cart road. The typhoon had wrought terrible havoc here. A forest seemed mowed down, helter-skelter. The path became steeper and rougher. Many natives passed by carrying great loads on their heads and shoulders. They were probably going to the pasar in Munduk.

Between clumps of trees and jungle growth, we had a continuous hide-and-seek view over the two ideally situated lakes from which the mountain slopes rose almost perpendicularly. Expansive woods covered the regions which seemed altogether unsuitable for cultivation. The Balinese imagined these little lakes to be populated with many goddesses. They had built little shrines dug deeply into the banks for the goddess Dewi Danua.

Near Tojo Ketipat, a path lead in the direction of Gitgit. We found a spring in a narrow pass, and a small sacred shrine to the goddess of Lake Buyan. Beyond this point, the path descended sharply; huge boulders and stones obstructed the way, and we had to pick our way carefully on this hazardous path. It was muddy, as many horses had made mush of this part of the trail. Lake Buyan was visible now and then during the descent, and it was equally as lovely as the two former ones. On the shore of this lake, in the shade of a number of tall jemara trees, stood a temple within which the goddess of Lake Buyan is supposed to dwell. It took us one-and-a-half-hours to climb from Munduk to the ridge between the lakes.

The most torturous downhill mountain trail we ever hiked was this last stretch. Worse than the steep part of the Bromo volcano climb, it took us three hours, down, down, down. Our legs trembled and our shoes almost broke. Just before Gitgit, we passed a small village ruined by the hurricane. Great trees had fallen and crushed dwellings. From here, we had a most marvelous panoramic view of Balinese landscape from the mountain down to the sea, with Java beyond. The scenery in Bali was not on such a grand scale as Java, but it was more intimate and therefore, to me, more lovely.

We arrived at Gitgit. It was perched on the steep mountain alongside a gravel road midst slopes of rice paddies and rushing streams, and overlooking a vast valley and sea below. We ate our lunch under a coconut palm and then continued to the cool and airy *pasangrahan*, which had been built at a vantage point for a fine view. We got mileage information to our next destination, which was Singaradja, ten kilometers ahead. We continued on foot as there were no buses available. At two P.M., we passed the little village of Lumbanan. We heard gamelan music and followed it to a community shelter, where we found the village had gathered and was watching a small girl being taught to dance and recite the classic plays. This teacher, a Balinese man, was grace itself, and an accomplished dancer. He exaggerated his movements in order to impress it upon his pupil. The village folk looked on approvingly. Gamelan music, played by three boys, accompanied the dancing, reciting, and singing. These classic plays have never been written, but are handed down from generation to generation in this way,

The next village on our route was the village of Sangket. There we found a village temple, Poera Desa. Under the community shelter, a full gamelan orchestra played. On a mat were two young boys of about twelve years interpreting music with dance movements. One youngster was a marvel. We thought his graceful arm, body and finger movements were excellent enough to have been a trained dancer. His pantomime was wonderful. The other boy seemed to be learning from him. Most of their dancing was done while on their knees. Their skill was evident not only in their arm and finger movements, but their whole upper body which they trained to bend in beautiful postures. On their knees most of the time, they rose halfway and sprang gracefully from one spot to another without changing leg positions. Every finger was trained in intricate movements, bending backwards, creating exquisite grace. Those small boys had wonderful mastery of their bodies enabling them to change from one angular position to another with lightening speed. No matter how closely we watched, their quick changes seemed to evade our eyes. Their faces remained expressionless except for the eyes. It was astonishing to see such trained dancers at this early age. Their costumes consisted of the everyday sarong, a long strip of material wound around the waist and forming a long skirt with the upper body exposed.

A famous Pura Desa was in the next village of Sukasado. This was an offering place with many shrines. The tallest shrine had eleven thatched roofs made beautifully green with moss. The temple gate was ornamental with bits of glass and colored plates stuck in for decoration. In the courtyard of the temple were several nicely-wrought figures of stone, weathered and softened by velvet green moss. There were grotesque statue figures resembling Javanese *wayang* figures. The pasar was next to the pura, as was usual in most villages here.

We next visited Beratan reputed to have the best artisans in Balinese silver work. We visited several silversmiths at work in shops alongside the road, and watched them tool the silver. They had models of clay and porcelain over which silver was molded and hammered to take on the same shape. The designs were of the same theme as the main designs in the temples.

Just before entering Singaradja proper, we inquired where Mr. Kowera's house was, as we had a letter to him from his son, Ida Moedra. We found him in a small mat bungalow. He greeted us graciously, and we gave him the letter from his son. We followed him across the street into a large private compound. His was a wealthy Balinese household. There were many buildings with doors of carved and painted wood and high floors with cement steps and porches. A shaded stream ran through the yard. However, no one spoke English or Dutch, so it was an awkward situation. He seemed to be waiting for his other son to awaken and interpret for him. He had a beautiful smile like his son Moedra. We felt we had to go, so we graciously left him and continued on our way to Singaradja, the capital of Bali.

Singaradja was beautiful, with gardens and blooming red Poinciana trees lining the clean orderly streets. Dutch tropical bungalows created a comfortable and lovely *pasangrahan*. There were rice paddies right in town.

There were many women along the road carrying temple offerings in carved and painted stands, and with ornamental baskets on their heads. They looked freshly bathed and dressed in their best sarongs with brilliant yellow and cerise scarves.

Buleleng, three kilometers from Singaradja, was a small squatty-looking town with Chinese and some Arab shops in a tawdry and cheap atmosphere with screeching phonographs, a lazy air, heat, mosquitoes, terrible hotels, and high prices. We stayed in a Malay hotel, which had the bathroom built above the flowing river, and had our meals in a Chinese restaurant.

We bought photos from a Chinese photo shop where the owner spoke good English. We thought he was a little naïve to say, "All Americans who travel have money." We convinced him we didn't. He was born in Java but his father came from Amoy, so we spoke to him of China. He sold us pictures at a reasonable rate saying that for us he charged a cheap price, but for rich tourists, who can pay more, he charged a bigger price.

At six thirty A.M., we took a dogcart to the village of Sangsit. It was a beautiful ride of about eight kilometers through rice terraces with mountains on one side and the sea on the other. The rice paddies seemed to extend to the shoreline. We were on a fine, paved road shaded by large trees. Sangsit seemed to be a sleepy little tropical town, stagnant and lazy, in contrast to the fresh early morning air. The mountains, we had climbed before, were to our right and, in the dim distance, the island of Java was discernible.

We went to the village to see an old temple which was well preserved and the most richly adorned temple in North Bali. The gateway groaned under its load of carved designs and figures, and here we could see the emergence of the ancient barbarism of the late Hindu period of the Balinese. The carved figures are monstrosities, grotesque, and threatening. They seem to represent the deities of the elements, the animals, and the unknown powers of the earth. This was the first time we saw a Balinese temple that actually had a real inner temple surrounded by an enclosed outer courtyard. Inside the enclosure, we saw several beautiful separate shrines to different gods. The grounds were nicely terraced and set with bas-relief. The climate of Bali quickly covered the stone with a green moss. It apparently aged even new structures. And this moss exquisitely mellows these old altars. The effect, as a whole, was beautiful in the inner enclosure. The outer entrance gate however was too grotesque for my liking. The main altar to *Suva*, in the inner courtyard, had a special altar top with roof beams of carved wood painted with gold leaf. We walked through the pasar, and then on to other temples of the village. One was Pura Dalam, (or temple of the dead), a popular offerings' place. The steps with carved statues were lovely.

Our next bus was to come at ten A.M. We waited at the pasar in a small Chinese stall, drinking tea and eating mangoes. The whole village seemed to be watching us from a market across the road. They tried to speak with us but without much success. Our bus arrived and we were on our way to our next destination of Kintamani.

Kintamani

Our bus went along the coast a few miles where we saw the temple of Kubutambahan, which was a typical temple grounds with walls, gateways, inner and outer courts. The bus turned directly southward cutting through the center of the island, and we climbed into the mountains again. The panoramic view at each turn of the road was marvelous. There were fewer villages here, for the region was barren and less cultivated than the western mountain section. The highest village, Kota Dalem, was reached at the mountain pass at 5,400 feet, and we had our first view of Lake Batur.

Kintamani had an elevation of 5,000 feet. It was a small village with a commanding view of the crater Batur, the peak of Bali, and Lake Batur. Glancing ahead and southward, we were overwhelmed by the magnificent panorama that stretched as far as the seacoast, and in the distance, Nusa Penida, which was once a convict isle.

On the ridge and rim of the lake, high above, laid Kintamani village where there was a large K.P.M. hotel and a smaller pasangrahan. This was indeed a unique spot because the highway was high enough to give us an opportunity to look into the crater of the still-smoking volcano Batur. We could hardly believe a road would be so close to a volcano that, as recently as 1926, had blown its peak and destroyed the surrounding villages and many lives. Several craters could be seen smoking on its slopes. It was a lovely but forbidding mountain. Its slopes were black with cinders and lava. Nothing grew for miles around it. Lake Batur, with barren shores, lay at the foot of the volcano. It was visible for three-quarters of a mile as the highway continued around the crater wall. We descended slightly to the village of Penelokan where a cutting in the hills showed an unrivaled panoramic view over the whole valley.

We took a bus to the next large village, Bangli. The K.P.M. hotel boy told us there was a new shortcut road from Bangli to Tirta Empul which eliminated the necessity of going down to Gianjar and back up again. So we got off at Bangli, which was still high in the hilly country, to visit the Poera Kehen temple. The grounds were stately with interesting pagoda-like structures of black grass roofs and decorated wooden pillars. There were some beautifully-carved and painted shelters with black thatch for roofs and bamboo platforms for sitting.

On to the pasar we went and made our purchases of bananas and other fruits. This village had several buildings about its square. There was a tall drum-tower at one corner with at least five hollowed logs hanging on ropes. Later we heard the beating of these drums from afar. We came to a small pavilion with carved pillars and beams and furnished with decorated armchairs covered with canvas. It looked like a small Balinese court of justice. We sat down to eat lunch and then went on our way, supposedly on the correct road (as we inquired from the natives) to Tirta Empul.

For a few hours we walked in what seems to us the wrong direction, as if we were going back in the same direction from which we came, only by another road, according to our compass. Time and time again we inquired of the natives, but often we could find out nothing except that Tirta Empul was further on. We saw very few villages. We passed vast rice fields of ripe grain, and a few orchards, sweet potato patches, and natives herding fine bulls. It was lovely pastoral scenery but the natives here seemed more wild looking, wore only scant loincloths, and longer hair, and some carried a curved knife in their belts. The natives couldn't understand us, or we them. By their surprise, we could see that they had seen few white people before. The road was beautifully shaded by a border of fine coconut palms. We went through the villages of Tija, Sakalah, and Tangahan Paket, still having Tirta Empul pointed out to us as just being in the near distance. We missed the right road, probably by not understanding the language. The short cut became a huge long cut, with us making a U-turn back in the direction from which we came. We walked at a quick pace trying to beat the darkness, but it closed in about us just the same. So, we continued our trek in the dark, not heeding where we stepped, if only to reach the pasangrahan that night sometime. At about seven P.M. a lovely native, whom we had earlier questioned, seemed to recognize the word pasangrahan, and voluntarily accompanied us for an hour, leading us past dark and silent kampongs.

A Balinese mountain village at night was usually dark and silent without a human stirring unless a fete was going on. At last, we crossed the river we knew was on the map. The native pointed up to a dim light on the hilltop, and we knew we had finally arrived at Tirta Empul and the pasangrahan after a hike of six hours instead of three! We paid the Balinese gratefully, for if not for him, we might have wandered a few hours more. The pasangrahan's caretaker was surprised to see us, so late at night, tired, dusty and footsore. I went to bed without even washing up as my legs just refused to hold me any more. Joe talked with the caretaker and learned he was born in Souraboya, so concluded that he must have some Malay blood. His wife and daughter also were Malasian. Voluntarily, he offered to charge us only two guilders for the room instead of the regular rate of four guilders for two people, which was another instance of kindness we experienced. (However he did not reduce the rate for Lee and Kane). We slept like dead ones and awoke to a fine morning, which revealed the magnificent view from the hilltop *pasangrahan* balcony. We saw the Pekrisan River and valley of rice terraces. Right below us was the sacred spring of Tirta Empul and its source. Tirta Empul was a sacred spot for the Balinese people and a popular pilgrimage spot all year long. Within the temple grounds, was a spring enclosed on four sides by a stone and mossy brick wall three feet high. This spring was held sacred and no one bathed in it. The sight of it bubbling up from the dark sand like a miniature volcano was beautiful. The spring had crystal clear water which was alive with fish and lovely green water plants growing around in the enclosure. This was the most beautiful spring we had ever seen. The water was channeled from the pool into the separate men's and women's baths where the flow came in a fine stream from the mouths of carved images. So prolific was this spring that its waters also filled a large swimming pool outside the temple grounds for the use of foreigners. There were many shrines and altars in the temple enclosure. One high piece of ground, about six feet by three feet, was covered with tall grass that was never touched. Balinese legend has it that angels were supposed to hover over this spot and it was, therefore, sacred. The caretaker of the pasangrahan explained many things. Then he pointed out the road to Tampaksiring, and we left him.

Tampaksiring was one mile over pleasant lanes. This place was noted for having beautiful Hindu relics. Off the main road, down steep rice paddies and into a deep rock canyon, we found old tombs and a rock convent of the early Hindus. On either side of the Pakrisan River were these monumental royal tombs hewn in the perpendicular rock walls of the canyon, just like temple gates. The name of this place was Gunung Kawi. There were five hewn-out tombs and a few roomy rock dwellings. Long ago these entrances probably could be closed from the inside by a wooden shutter. The sight was one of remarkable natural beauty with the river rushing over boulders at our feet. We would have liked to linger here all day!

We went back to the road again and found the native pasar in full swing. We purchased excellent bananas, a papaya, coconut, small cakes and fried peanuts, and sat down in one sitting to breakfast and lunch, with half of the village watching us, as usual.

Bedhulu

We decided to take the next bus to Gianyar, but a taxi driver made us a fair price, so we piled in and rode to the vicinity of Bedhulu where there was a remarkable structure called *Pura Goa Gadjah*. This was a pagan shrine or a Ciwaistie temple which dated back to the twelfth or thirteenth century. It was underneath the highway and rather difficult to find if one did not know about it, as it was completely hidden from view. This temple was actually a cave, the entrance of which was the open mouth of a huge giant forcing his way out through the wall. The relief carvings represented people and animals making their hurried escape in anger and terror.

Beneath the "monster," in the form of a cross, we found access to a subterranean passage inside. The walls contained niches in which a few images were still to be seen, and offerings were still placed before them. The relief work on the outside, the monsters face and its huge gaping mouth, was weather-beaten but still formed an interesting sight for a historical study. It was too grotesque to be beautiful, but it arrested our attention just because of its barbaric ugliness.

We continued, in the same taxi, to the next interesting spot in the vicinity which was called *Toja Pulu*. This was a most beautiful rock sculpture about two meters high and thirty meters long. We met a native boy who guided us to the spot from the road — down and between rice terraces, over streams, and up again over terraces over little frail bridges. It took us fifteen to twenty minutes to get there. At one point, this little fellow carried a huge stone almost as big as he and placed it in the middle of a rice paddy stream so we could cross without taking off our shoes and socks. Another time, he warned us to wait, and we saw a snake glide by and lose itself in the rice.

The bas-relief sculptured out of the solid rock was a rare example of old Hindu art undiluted by Balinese animism. It represented a hunting scene with figures of men, women, horses, boars and tigers. Water trickled down over the sculpture from the rice paddies above. It was a beautiful piece of work in its simplicity of line and form; set out by itself, surrounded by hilly rice fields, and bathed with continuously dripping water from a bubbling spring. This piece of art had a most lovely setting. We felt that it was in such settings of nature that works of art should be seen and kept.

We arrived at Gianyar, a fair-sized village, and on this day a busy bazaar and fair were in full swing. This village was the center of wood carving, gold and silver work, and brass industries of Bali. The population was centered in the southeastern part of the island where the influential princes, "the Rajah's of Klungkung," ruled in the past years. The western part of the island was mostly a mountain waste district, and almost uninhabited.

We piled into a bus going to Klungkung. It had the liveliest and busiest market we had seen in Bali. Vendors and their articles were jammed against each other until hardly any room was left to pass through. We picked our way over crocks of food and squatting women, purchased some fruit, and made arrangements for another bus.

This was a beautiful place since it had a park square with flowers and tree-shaded roads. At one corner of the aloon stood a platform called the *Kerta Gossa*, an ancient Balinese court of justice which was similar to the one we saw in Bangli only more beautifully decorated. We climbed to the raised stone floor on steps bordered with carved images. The pillars supporting the roof were intricately carved and decorated with gold leaf and colors. The raised bas-relief of the floor was decorated beautifully, and there were many lovely carved chairs with a table in the center of the platform. All this was simply amazing, but the main interest was in the ceiling and wall decorations. The decorated ceiling beams were carved, and extended into a sunburst pattern. All of this was hand-decorated with beautiful drawings, painted scenes, and figures that reminded us of Javanese wayang figures. The effect was like a delicate Persian drawing. This was the first time we had seen any Balinese art that resembled the Javanese.

The drive between Klungkung and Krang-Asam was one of the loveliest on the island. We skirted the coast for many miles, climbed mountains, and saw grand vistas of sea and coconut palm crests nestled between mountains and the sea below, with the isle of Nusa Penida always in sight. We had the ocean and the pounding surf with us the whole drive. It was one of the most pleasant trips we had.

The buses in Bali had no set price, so we had to bargain with the drivers. On the bus was a group of refined Balinese. One little girl of ten spoke perfect Dutch. She had a beautiful face as did her two sisters and brother. She nestled against me like a kitten curious as to my clothes, hair, and skin, but she was reserved and delicate. She told us her father worked in a secretariat in the Radhuis, next door to the pasangrahan of Karang-Asam.

The pasangrahan was expensive, but not very nice. We decided not to pay their prices. We took our packs and set out for the center of the town not knowing where we should sleep that night, for there were no hotels.

Karang Asam was beautifully situated. One could see the sea six kilometers away, and behind the town rose the perfect peak of Bali. It reminded us of a Swiss village in its setting and rushing water. We arrived near the pasar, which was empty, and found a small Chinese restaurant that wasn't any too clean. We told the manager that there were no more buses back to Den Pasar that night. We told him that the pasangrahan had been full (which was not true). He offered us his upstairs, which was one big room with two windows, and was furnished with two dirty mattresses, on boxes, covered with matting. It was dusty and musty there, but airy enough, and he assured us there were no mosquitoes. He busied himself with sweeping a bit, while he fixed a special nook partitioned off with matting for Tonia. The bed had two fresh clean sheets, two pillows, with embroidered cases, and a Dutchman (pillow).

We had a Chinese dinner downstairs in the little restaurant and then took a walk through the half-dark village. Small kerosene lamps lit the shops and stands. The manager gave us two kerosene lamps as we went upstairs. We put up our mosquito netting and slept soundly. There were big rats, so we hung our provision basket from a bamboo pole. The bed was hard but bearable, and we let the kerosene lamp burn low all night. Downstairs, the Chinese manager reclined while smoking opium and drinking coffee all night. He alternated his water pipe, with cigarettes, coffee, and opium.

We got up at four A.M. dressed and packed, wishing to hike the four kilometers to Udjung. The manager's shrewdness became evident the next morning when asked him the rate for the garret sleeping quarters. He laughed and said it was not good enough for white people, and he wouldn't take anything for it. But then he charged us enormous prices for food. In the morning we didn't order a breakfast, but only tea, and he, up to his tricks, charged us half a guilder for a pot. When we got ready to leave, he asked for four guilders for the room. We refused flatly, since we hated to be made a fool of or taken advantage of. We did intend to pay him a reasonable amount for the room, but because of his actions over the food bill, we gave him nothing. However, he made plenty on the food alone.

Five A.M. we were on the road hiking to Udung where the pleasure palaces and gardens of the regent are at sea level. The calm and peaceful gardens were lovely with little pools and lakes and pavilions rising from the water. Some of the pavilions looked Chinese. They seemed forlorn and deserted even though they were still tended by gardeners. A river ran outside the wall of the garden which was on a gentle slope from the sea. The boys undressed on the rocky beach and went for a dip. No beach in Bali was nice for it was either too rocky or full of coral reefs. At this time, the native outriggers were coming in from their night of fishing. They beached their craft and carried all their gear and their catch of brilliantly colored fish to their huts.

On our way to and from Udjung, we saw the 1,200 foot peak, Gunung Agung, in a fine clear and majestic setting, rising up like Mount Fuji crowned to a perfectly coned crater. This part of Bali was covered with beautiful terraces of rice paddies and rushing streams.

Puri was the regent's little city within the larger one of Karan-Asam. The main royal quarters were walled in. One section was open, so we walked in and found a series of courtyards, carved gateways, and gravel walks shaded by great trees behind the outer street wall. Within was a lovely pool of water facing the public audience hall. A Chinese-like pavilion in the center of the pool connected the outer walks by small bridges. The deeply-carved and gilded doors of the audience hall were also Chinese in design. An air of dignity and peace was present within the walls of the garden while many craftsmen squatted on the porches or under shelters chiseling out new stone figures for the temples or carving beautiful designs in wood. In front of the pond was a fine aviary of colorful birds.

On the street again, the route became a paved, narrow gravel path rising into the mountains. The native kampong of Puri was up this road. A fine canal lined the street in the Karang-Asam. At about ten thirty A.M., we changed to another bus going to Den Pasarack. The bus, as usual, was loaded with people, bananas, boxes, tires, iron, goats and personal gear. A jolly crowd of Balinese, laughed, joked and ate fruit during that trip.

We arrived in Den Pasar at midday, and felt the damp scorching heat. We were nearly at sea level there, and felt it. There were four hotels in the town: the Bali, run by the K.P.M., Satrya, run by the Germans, and two hotels run by Chinese. We located a small Malay restaurant and ordered tea, got our bearings and cooled off.

To our surprise, in walked our friend Hartman whom we had met in Honolulu a few months earlier. He had come back to Bali. He looked terrible! He was nervous, and feverish, having been sick with fever for the past three weeks. Just talking made him nervous, and put him in a sweat. We learned then that the Dutch resented foreigners going about in shorts and eating in native restaurants as one bawled out Hartman in Dutch.

We stopped at Su Ankie at a new Chinese hotel which was neat and clean. Early the next morning, we took a dogcart to Sanur to visit Hartman. We met his companion Allen Bledsoe, a Southern boy, who was quite a bit younger. We spent the most enjoyable day and the most peaceful and companionable day we had had for a month, since we had been with our ill-chosen traveling companions, Kane and Lee.

Sanur was just a tiny fishing village of a few huts and many outrigger canoes. The house in which Hartman stayed was large and comfortable. Two American friends of his, an artist and his wife, rented it from a Dutchman. They had gone to French Indo-China and left him with the house and servants. Balinese servants lived on the premises and worked in the garden and yard. Hartman showed us his collection of Balinese art, which included paintings on cambric of the Hindu legends, wood carvings, temple masks and ornaments, fans and other woven materials. He had a delicate taste for color and texture and understood good line and craftsmanship.

We enjoyed the conversation and learned many things from him, as he was a sympathetic and an artistic natural. We draped sarongs and tried on dancing headdresses. We were shown one purple silk couch cover of gold leaf appliqué which was used only once in a boy's life when he came of age. Dressed in his finest robes, he reclined on a couch covered with such a piece of silk, and endured the process of having his lower teeth filed down evenly. This stamped him as an adult.

We had a simple but tasty lunch of fresh cooked vegetables which was a treat in these parts. After lunch, Joe and I took a walk to a nearby kampong to view a beautiful pura which was carved out of white coral rock. Set amidst the palms the lines of its entrance gate were lovely — simple and free of over-ornamentation. Inside was a fine bas-relief on coral screen. It was one of the loveliest temples we had seen in Bali, but it wasn't listed or shown in the guidebook.

The next morning we walked to Pandhuis to look for Balinese materials. We went into a native hut and watched a woman who was weaving cloth. A tremendous amount of work was put into these Balinese sarongs. It was a pity that very bad dyes were used on the thread which made them run in hot water. Their silver and gold weaves, and some of their rougher cottons with silk, were lovely. But the ordinary-looking weaves were not worth the effort. A machine-made weave would be far more satisfactory and beautiful. White thread was imported from America and England, dyed with German dyes before it was woven into cloth. I have seen better woven cloths in other lands done on a hand loom.

Many children had white rice powder smeared over their foreheads and faces as a remedy for the heat. They looked quite ghost-like and fantastic. The adults smeared a yellow vegetable ointment over their bodies which acted as a skin lotion rendering the body a mustard color. But, it would wash off. A greenish paste (concocted of herbs) was smeared on the forehead or in round dots on the temples as remedies for various aches. Bracelets of twisted black root made from a sea plant were worn by men as a protection against rheumatism.

We took a bus to Sukawati, which was about fourteen kilometers from Den Pasar, to see a very old temple. Inside the gateway part of a stone screen still stood, and carved on it in an excellent bas relief was the first and only screen dealing with every day human life we had seen in Balinese temples. The scene depicted rice sheaves, straw hats, and a farmer plowing with a water buffalo. It was a masterful piece of art. The temple as a whole was a pleasing sight.

We walked through the pasar at a busy time. It was filled with pottery, matting, corn, betel nut articles, fruit, and beans. We looked at some Balinese woven sarongs. Boys stitched up the sarongs with sewing machines as people bought them. The village had beautiful shaded roads, so we sat under a tree and had lunch. Four little, naked boys, watched our every move until we finished. We walked back, and passed three boys practicing gamelan under a shelter house. It was noon, and many people were stretched out on bamboo floors or benches in the shelters.

We hailed a bus. It was filled with a colorful medley of people: good-looking Balinese, Chinese in fine garments, a few Arabs, and two pure white goats tied to the rear seat bars.

We got off at Kesiman to see another interesting old pura. At the corner of the road was a temple-like courtyard and a large house in which a native Rajah lived. Access to the temple was hidden, and a small, beautiful Balinese boy ran ahead leading us through narrow lanes, back yards, and over high gates, into the temple courtyard itself. The tranquility of this temple was extraordinary, unlike any others. It was surrounded by a deep moat of water with a pavilion rising from the center in the water which formed an inner moat. A tall, obelisk shrine rose at one side from the back. It was carved out of white material that looked like white coral rock.

A group of small boys joined us as we sat on the steps of the pavilion. Much of the carved work was cut out of the red brick used for the altars. This, Kisiman pura was the loveliest we had yet seen in Bali. Its mossy, red brick, mossy green water, and its quietness and seclusion seemed so much of a part of Bali.

We made our way out, purchased some bananas from a young woman vendor, and placed six Chinese coins in the surprised hand of our little guide. His smile and surprise was beautiful. We were hunting for fan-makers, and instead, we found the abode of women who sold Bali crafts and clothes. Young boys showed us a large collection, but we purchased nothing.

When any entertainment is scheduled in a Balinese kampong, whoever is nearby or hears about it is welcome to come. Balinese customs of entertaining are the same as their customs of hospitality, of community work, and of communal temple feast days. All members of the village share equally in everything — play, work, dance, and music. To witness a real Balinese dance, or a wayang puppet show, was to get an insight into the everyday life of these lovable people.

Our little room boy, in the small Chinese hotel in Den Pasar, knocked on our door one night, after we had fallen asleep, to tell us there was a wayang in one of the nearby kampongs. We dashed into our clothes like children going to a circus. A wayang? Where was it? Which way? It was eleven-thirty at night, and a wayang was in progress somewhere down behind the pasar. We hurried down the deserted streets as the boy shouted and waved his arms to show where we should turn. It was pitch dark as we left the main street behind the pasar, and we walked for quite a while with rough gravel under our feet. Not a sound could be heard nor a light seen. We began to think we had been awakened for nothing, for surely we ought to have heard the music, the laughter, and the buzz of the audience, or some lights to guide us. Instead of turning back, we continued further up this lane just to see if anything was going on, though we were almost positive that we wouldn't find anything. But we were rewarded by a dim light in the distance and greeted by a chorus of those most woe-begotten, vicious dogs of Bali, setting up an awful howl. Then we found ourselves in a kampong community square, and there the wayang was going on. The courtyard was filled with Balinese, young and old together, under the stars, beneath the shelters, standing, sitting and squatting and grouped around the sides of the shadow screen. Little kerosene lamps gave the only light to the yard, as they were perched on the small stands of the vendor women. The vendors were selling peanuts, cool drinks, betel nuts, and portions of cooked foods on banana-leaf plates. It was a rather quiet audience, but one that was vastly interested in what was going on against the lit screen located at one end of the yard. It seemed to be a friendly audience. The few who could see us, in the dim flickering light, smiled that we were also enjoying this with them. The wayang had been set up under a shelter that had been raised about three feet above the floor. A white screen had been stretched between the front posts. On this screen, the animated figures of the puppets moved about acting out the ancient Hindu legend of the Ramayana. They were perfect little shadow figures.

Here was a Balinese story far older than our Western shadow screen plays. Behind the screen was the workshop. The voices were the soul and music of the show as the puppets were given life and animation. It looked complicated to us from the front, so we went around to the back of the screen. We saw one man manipulating these puppets, speaking lines, singing, shouting, and weeping for them. He sat crossed-legged on the floor immediately behind the white screen. A large bowl-shaped petrol lamp flared just in front of his head. Silent helpers sat on either side of him handing him the figures in their order of appearance. He was the only one that worked them, handling as many as four and five at one time. Some were flat against the screen and others moved and disappeared as the story went on. He even held a piece of metal in his right toe which he banged against a wooden board for certain effects. This puppet man's declaiming (reciting) was really marvelous. It reminded us of the declaiming of the main actors in a Japanese puppet show — even to the voice intonations, the sing-song crying, and the wails of woe. He acted out each part behind the screen as if he had an audience right before him — and not just the puppets. Two boys sat over muted gamelans playing whenever the little puppets entered or left the screen. It was remarkable how the figures were made to come to life. Their arms moved, and some of them opened and closed their mouths as they talked. We went to the front again and watched for a long time. The flare of the torch showed through the screen. Adding to the weirdness and beauty of the shadows the wayang figures looked like gods with heads of fire.

These puppets were similar to the wayang puppets of Java. The puppets were cut from buffalo hide, intricately tooled, and cut out in lace-like patterns. The arms were joined at the shoulder and the elbows. A stick to move them was attached at the wrists. A long stick was joined to the body to manipulating it. For animal and demon characters, the lower jaw of the mouth was made moveable by a string attached and operated by one finger. These puppets were flat and did not look so fine at first sight as the doll-shaped puppets of other lands. But their beauty emerged against an illuminated screen. The finely-cut designs were magnified as the costumes assumed life, and intricate ornaments of headdress and jewelry came alive. What was just a flat piece of buffalo hide, beautifully designed and cut out, became a living character of the Ramayana and the life of Buddha. Someone was celebrating, and this wayang was given for the whole kampong. We remained until two A. M. and the festivities were still going on. Thus, one happens upon the Bali ways at all hours. We just had to scout around, and accidentally find these Balinese shows, for they were not announced. They were given when the occasion came up, or so it seemed. We found more going on in an hour's walk through a small village than we would find in days of inquiring and waiting perhaps in a larger town.

This wayang was an example of how the Balinese enjoyed themselves. They laughed at the comical situations, and took sides with the puppet's battles. And these puppets could battle, flinging themselves all over the screen, stabbing with swords and lances. People flung down Chinese cash (1/6 of a Dutch one-cent piece), and munched the tidbits they had purchased. Some of the young children fell asleep in their parents' arms. Then a sudden rain squall sent everyone scurrying for shelter, but the show continued just the same. After the rain ceased, the people continued watching the screen, eating, and softly chatting. No one was loud or rowdy. A more refined audience would be hard to find. The puppets, the stage, the musical gamelans, were all made by the very people watching the wayang. They all knew these classic tales by heart, yet never tired of them. We left them in the dim kampong while the shadow figures danced across the screen like filigreed bits of animation into the early hours of the dark morning. We could not keep awake any longer. We stumbled back over the dark, paved lane to our little hotel. The boy had not locked up entirely. He kept a small door open for us to squeeze in.

In Den Pasar, the hotel management had commercialized Balinese entertainment for the tourists. Each Friday night, on the lawn in front of the Bali hotel, a so-called, typical Balinese entertainment was given. It was gamelan music and dancing for the tourist guests of that hotel. They paid big prices to the hotel for it. We witnessed part of one and left before it was finished. The first part which featured a young girl dancing was good. Then a man dancer came, and they danced together. We felt they put on a cheap burlesque. Western comedic jokes and antics at which the natives, looking on from the street, booed and jeered. That man dancer was capable of dancing skillfully, but he made a terrible mess of it by doing what the Chinese guides, and the hotel manager told him to do, since he was paid by them. To give music and dancing for money is basically against Balinese custom and ways. Their entertainment was gratis for the kampongs and given for the sheer enjoyment of creating, or of religious custom. One senses that the unspoiled Balinese would not give his best performance for money.

We left and joined the gamelan players whose shelter was not far from the hotel. We went many evenings to hear them practice. Once we found them playing with a gusto that comes from the sheer love of performing while natives and vendors in the area enjoyed listening. A young man danced with beautiful arm movements, while kneeling most of the time, and performing adroit leaps with crossed bent legs, springing from one spot to another. It was graceful but a difficult thing to do. The musicians and some vendors already knew us, since we had often listened to them. The Balinese seemed to sense that we truly enjoyed their music and dance. If they saw that you truly liked it, they would play their hearts out for you.

It was great to find such a small island of beautiful people which had a unique culture of its own. Bali is noticeably a land of women — about 70%. Balinese women apparently had more freedom than Javanese women, in that they often chose their own husbands. The women's costume was neither Hindu nor Javanese for they went bare above the waist. Their sun-browned beautiful figures blended in with the soft browns and yellows of their sarongs. They walked with a swinging, easy gait, straight as an arrow and supple as a willow tree from years of balancing burdens on their heads. All day long we noticed the slender and graceful figures with beautifully chiseled faces. Without exception, I believe they are, as a whole, the most beautiful native women in the world.

The women, most of whom were weavers, not only did all of the carrying and building, but ;they also performed most of the labor of the island except in the rice fields. There, the men reigned supreme. The men were experts in managing their marvelous system of irrigation.

The landscape seemed to be a continual succession of "pocket handkerchief" rice fields. They were in all stages of growth, from the young green of the sprouting rice, to the golden brown stubble of the harvested grain. After it was cut, the rice is neatly tied in small bunches and carried home by the women in large baskets on their heads, and by the men on shoulder poles.

Everywhere, there was the spirit of helping each other. There were no beggars, and only a few prisoners on the island. We saw no signs of strife, contention, or dire poverty. When one man's rice crop was ready, all the neighbors helped until the crop was harvested. And so in turn, they helped each other.

The Balinese were a curious and interesting people, widely different from other native races we had met. They were highly artistic with an inherited charming devotion to an old faith. Almost every one of them, it seemed, was a musician and knew the good features of the dance. Of course, they grew their rice for their own sustenance, but even in that, it seemed to be a religious duty to give offerings to the rice fields every week in the year.

A Hindu temple was built and dedicated to the gods of mythology and to the spirits of the hills and the trees. Almost daily, the Balinese temples were thronged with natives in festive dress, freshly bathed and hair neatly combed, bearing offerings to the god of the rice or the sun, in thankful recognition of their prosperity. And, of what did their prosperity consist? They needed so little! Instead of striving to build fine mansions or amass fortunes, the native Balinese were content with humble, thatched-roofed houses of plaited bamboo enclosed in mud or stone walls, and with small private temples showing above the wall along the road.

Each month, every man contributed his share of earnings towards the upkeep of his immediate neighborhood temple. So, instead of an individual profiting in Bali, religion profited. The building of artistic temples to the gods was the height of every man's zealous ambition. The sweet, kindly simplicity of their faith and their customs create the charm of Bali. No matter how small the village, there was a temple in some beautifully wooded spot, always with the characteristic painted Balinese gateway with carved stone Hindu images and statues.

The life of the Balinese was composed of one religious ceremony after another. The temples offering ceremonies were a daily phenomenon. Gamelan bells pealing their plaintive tune could be heard from afar. One could very often see stately files of youthful bronzed-goddesses bearing tall bowls on their heads, all intricately fastened together in a cone shape. At a large offering, one could see as many as three hundred young women or maidens carrying their bright gifts to the gods. We saw so many beautiful things, all the time in Bali that one wanted to take pictures constantly. It was quite remarkable that no one objected or seemed to take notice as we stood and gaped at their ceremonies. Rather, they seem pleased that we should care to witness their temples of which they are very proud. They kept on repeating the word "bagus," meaning beautiful.

Of course, cremation was the most tremendous ceremony in Bali. The cremation altars, or *wadahs*, were picturesque, many tiered structures of light wood, in which to lay the body. According to the number of tiers in the *wadah*, it was evident to which caste the deceased belonged. These tiers mounted as high as nine tiers in the cremation of royalty.

The men were not bothered with the task of carrying burdens. If it was not time to plant, harvest, or cultivate their rice, they either gambled the day away, or tended to their precious fighting cocks. (Fighting roosters apparently, was more important to them than was their wives.) Everywhere, beside the small cottages, we could see the round baskets in which a cock was often kept for two years before it was allowed to participate in a festive fight. But every day the bird was taken from his basket by his master and carefully washed, groomed, and his joints massaged. Then tender tidbits were fed to him.

Cock fighting was a passion with the Balinese, and often as much as two hundred gilders were bet on a fight between two choice specimens. Formerly, the cocks were doubly armed for the fray with a tiny razor-sharp, steel-knife on the right spur. These little knives were even smeared with deadly poisonous oil.

We watched them with curiosity. There were many cages. One man took out his most beautiful bird, smilingly held it up to us, and stroked its feathers. Two men would let their cocks go after each other. Their neck feathers would ruffle up as the men held them back by their tails. Cocks were the prize pets of Bali. A man often had a dozen or more, and took them out from their special cages a few times each day for them to pick grass. Each afternoon the grass borders of the roadsides were filled with cocks and their owners. It seemed to be a regular industry in Bali and one of the bigger ones.

Cock fighting was actually prohibited by the government, except at certain times of the year. Nevertheless, fights were held secretly.

Betting and gambling ran riot at these fights. A man would bet his wife and house away on his cock.

We spoke with many Dutchmen in the islands who spoke with disdain about the Sumatran and Balinese. "They are not good for anything but to loaf. They need a good kicking to come to that realization. We are forced to take Javanese help with us when going to their islands, because the Balinese and Sumatrans make bad servants."

The very things we found beautiful about these natives, the Dutch detested. They used mild methods to kill the free spirit in the Balinese. Individually, they were forced to cover their naked bodies with Javanese jackets. (I am convinced, in a few years, Balinese native life will become as dull as that of the Javanese.)

The Balinese were not business people, and did not care to complicate their simple and contented life. Whereas, the Chinese had a good nose for money and exploited the Balinese. The Chinese decided to do the business for the Balinese, and wherever there was room enough for a store, a Chinese would move in. A Brahmin Balinese boy told me, "The Chinese and the Arabs in Bali are the bloodsuckers of the island. They become richer while the natives get poorer." He also mentioned, "One can see a Chinaman come to Bali in short trousers and penniless, and after few years he has a well-established store, nice home, and has become a rich man."

Kompong, Kedaton, noted for its excellent temple dancers was two kilometers from Den Pasar. Ever since tourists began coming to Den Pasar, each Saturday morning from eight to ten had been set aside for performances by these famous Balinese dancers. That same day, many temples were being decorated with palm fringes, woven palm hangings, and fresh white flags for the big offering next day.

As we walked to Kedaton, we saw fresh bamboo poles in every community square. Men and boys were busily cooking and preparing the feast for the morrow. The brick ovens were hot, smoke wafted up from the roofs, and fragrant odors filled the air. Under one shelter, squatting in a double row, were perhaps twenty men and boys cracking and grating fresh coconut. Under another, they were taking cooked meat off the bones and chopping it very fine. Meat, for soup, was cooked in great clay pots. One boy presided over a pot frying peanuts and beans, flavored with special green leaves. Other men were stirring great bowls which contained a mixture of the coconut pulp, green and red hot peppers, salt, onions, and various other morsels. This was tested by winding a bit of it at the end of a small bamboo stick and searing it over a charcoal fire to broil it. One man made one especially for me, and it was very tasty. A huge basket of shredded banana and bamboo sprouts, looking like sliced onions, was being mixed with oil, peppers, salt, and spices. Every kampong had such a scene early on that morning.

The dogs were crazy from the smell of food, and they fought over the bones. By ten A.M., the activity was over and everything cleared up. And in its place, the men were sitting with the sticks lined up in front of them, broiling them over long rows of charcoal and hot ashes. One of the young boys gave me a beautifully marked piece of tortoise shell cut into a fan.

The day was terribly hot as we walked back to Den Pasar. At the hotel we undressed and tried to sleep through midday. We were soaked with perspiration the whole time. It was just impossible to do anything.

Kriss Dance:

At four P.M., we walked to the cemetery to see the celebration of the day — a Kriss Dance. Under a shelter, in the compound, were four boys being dressed in white costumes with smiling masks. Many women walked about bringing fresh food and flower offerings to the temple. A Balinese priest sat in a palm hut before a carved statue of the guardian god of the temple. Offerings were given to the priest. He blessed them while saying a prayer and held them up to the idol. He sprinkled scented water over the offerings and placed them before the idol. The women and girls were in their finest, freshly washed, sarongs. All of them wore brilliant flowing scarves. The boys came into the courtyard, and knelt before a priest. Incense burned in a coconut shell. Flower-infused scented-water was handed to the priest, who was assisted by young girls as he blessed and sprinkled the water over the boys' hands to consecrate them before the dance. A lesser priest stood aside holding a large open umbrella. The bowl of incense was then placed before each boy as he tried to capture the smoke with his hands and breathe it. The huge lion-costumed figure, that was to dance, also came before the priest for blessings. All the children had fragrant blossoms arranged in their hair dangling on their foreheads. Special water was poured on the ground while prayers were said during this ceremony. Then a small rice offering was placed on the ground. A dog, snatched it and devoured it, but no one molested it or took notice. After these ceremonies were finished, the music began, and the dancers filed out into the thronged outer courtyard under the great banyan trees,

The gamelan orchestra played. Small stands were set up with their trays of peanuts or drinks. The village folk filed into the yard in groups, and the four little boys began dancing. They wore fine masks, depicting a kind smiling character, and enacted an ancient Balinese and Hindu mythological story. A fifth dancer entered the circle. Then five or six other characters came in, all masked and costumed to represent devils, demons, a grinning one-eyed man (a master of pantomime), a dumb-head, and several lion-headed monsters with horrible long fingernails. The age-old stories of triumph of good over evil, dark superstitious beliefs of wild devils and good spirits were enacted under the trees. The devils often ran up to the spellbound children, who were watching, and they would squeal in fright, and then everybody laughed.

These boys worked themselves into frenzy until they trembled like leaves. An evil spirit was supposed to be possessing them. The music and the people became wild. As the boys got up, curved-bladed krisses (or swords) were placed in their hands by the priests. They began to chase wildly after the demon figure, called Rangda, which had a hairy head and long nails. Back and forth they ran — either after the demon or the demon after them. They became so infuriated and possessed that sometimes a boy had to be held by the priest to prevent injury to the demon.

The music became wild, the cries of the people wilder, and to our horror, we saw these boys and men sticking the daggers into themselves while uttering wild cries. They worked themselves into such frenzy that they didn't feel the points in their chests. The priests wrenched the kriss away from each, just at the right moment before the shouting dancer could do himself harm. Some rolled wildly on the ground shouting and waving their arms, and actually had to be held down by the priests. After all the krisses had been retrieved, each boy ran to the priest with a shout, throwing himself into the priest's arms, and kissed the forehead of the lion figure standing by. Some of them fell exhausted onto the ground; some still continued to rave. It was almost dark when it finished, and we were sick and trembling from seeing such a barbaric sight. The crowd dispersed, and we walked back along the roadway, weak in the knees.

At eight thirty that same night, not far from the Bali hotel, we saw a fine Legong dance given by the Balinese gamelan orchestra, and danced by two exquisite little dancers about age nine. This dance was far better and more complete than the one we saw that morning at Kedaton. It was given for their own enjoyment and not for tourists. Vendors and natives crowded around, intently interested, and enjoying it all. These young dancers had beautiful little bodies swathed tightly in costly garments. They were as lithe as reeds and their hand and finger movements were marvelously intricate. They were simply splendid. Such a highly developed dance technique was rarely achieved by older dancers.

This same gamelan orchestra had become used to our presence, as we had listened to their practicing and playing from beginning to end every evening. They appreciated our listening and enjoying their music. At the end each night, some of them always came to tell us what they would have the next night.

We walked to the hotel our minds filled with what we had seen during the day and evening. Close to eleven PM., we heard the distant gongs of the gamelan again. It was a clear, starry night and distant lightening lit our way. The few natives we passed on the road greeted us. We finally found the spot, and just as we came to the open square, the music ceased, — finished for the night!

The musicians felt sorry and told us that on the next night would be another one. We walked back to the hotel, having enjoyed the walk in the dark while listening to the distant music. By midnight, we were in bed. We went to sleep, tired but spiritually happy.

Next morning, we decided to take a bus to Negara and we left Den Pasar in a near empty bus. For once we had enough leg room, but being empty, the bus bounced about so that we got a terrible shaking, and Tonia got a blister at the end of her spine.

The bus kept climbing from Den Pasar to Badjra in the mountains. At Badjra, someone called to us. We turned and, lo-and-behold, it was our 'Brahmin' friend, Moedra. He was so overjoyed to see us that he didn't know what to say. He took my basket and bananas and ate a banana without even knowing it. This was the village in which he was stationed, and he implored us to remain the rest of the day. We could stay overnight with him and continue tomorrow. We too, were glad to see him again. We let Kane and Lee go on with the bus while we remained behind in Badjra. Moedra told us he drove to Singaragia the day we were there, to see us after we left him in Poejoengan, but found we had already left for Kintamani. Moedra related all this as we went toward his house and courtyard. There, we met his wife, who was not as lovely and beautiful as most Balinese women we had seen. She was beginning to chew betel nut.

Moedra brought fresh socks and trousers for Joe. He gave me a fresh sarong. He seemed to know what to do for our comfort. Soon we three took a long hike over the mountain road to a beautiful look-out point. There was a splendid view of the sea, mountains, rice terraces, and the South tip of Bali called Texelhuk. Moedra had brought a new cake of soap and fresh towel. Beside us ran a swift stream beneath ferns and trees. First I bathed and then the two men. We sat barefooted on the grass after bathing and felt so glad to be together again. We walked back to Badjra where we had first met our friend weeks ago.

In Badjra, we visited a little while with a dear friend of Moedra's, a Balinese of the second caste, or Vesya, and his beautiful young wife. The women of the courtyard, and various little houses around Moedra, had prepared a sumptuous lunch for us three, but poor Joe nearly inflamed his mouth and throat on the fiery lombok (or peppers) that flavor every Balinese dish. Moedra felt so badly about it!

We met Moedra's brother, a beautiful man with a fine sense of humor, who spoke perfect Dutch and Malay. He was eighteen, and had his own ideas. He said he didn't want to associate with people who were exceptionally strong in physique and usually stupid mentally. He didn't want to grow fat as the brain became sluggish and lost it sharpness. He was a born proud son of Bali, a true son of the sun! He wanted to own rice fields instead of useless fine houses.

In the courtyard, women dyed threads for the hand-woven sarongs, dried them and then reeled them onto spools. Moedra had some work to do, writing and figuring, so we had our afternoon nap in their little bedroom. I put on a fresh sarong. The house had a dirt floor and the bed had fresh linen, which was draped with figured cotton for a mosquito net. Another bamboo framed bed stood alongside this bed. Later, Moedra's wife and his brother came in for awhile, and talked.

That night was still a Balinese holiday, and a village dance and gamelan orchestra was scheduled to play. We woke up from our nap about six, and had supper on the porch. The food was not so peppery this time. We gave Moedra an English lesson, as he was very anxious to begin to learn. He was an apt and eager pupil. He brought out his guitar and tried to play. He wanted to learn and do so many things. He strove to wrench out whatever he could of the world from his little spot in Bali.

A quick storm with heavy rain and wind came up while we were eating. It lasted all night, so we sat on the porch with the flickering kerosene lamp and talked. His brother removed his sarong and walked about in red shorts, with a big umbrella over him. He carried dishes from one hut to another and from the outside kitchen to their supper table. They joked and laughed. Rain didn't bother them. A woman friend made a special Balinese green vegetable dish, and gave each of us a serving. The older women rubbed the bodies of the young children with fragrant tree balm and oils to keep them warm. We talked far into the night about Balinese customs, and Moedra explained many things about Balinese cremation:

*****

Every Balinese begins saving money when he is young for his own and his family's cremation. He will skimp on food, and save every cent in anyway possible. The cheapest *cremation costs $1,000 gold. Bali has no institutional church with a bank account. Religion, like its art, had not yet become a business.*

The cremation is a great feast, and hordes of guests are invited to the house. The gamelan orchestras are hired, and besides their playing fees, they must also be fed for at least twenty days. The Wadah costs two hundred dollars gold. Priests are paid for special ceremonies, and gifts given to the temple. All in all, it is very expensive. Therefore, a family can have no more than one cremation in one generation. So the corpses are held sometimes for years, awaiting the time for the cremation when enough money has been carefully saved. Some bury the dead for years, and then dig them up for the cremation. Others keep them in the houses and slowly dry or embalm the bodies. Only the first six months is there an offensive odor.

*****

Moedra told us he had a grandfather in his father's house awaiting cremation, and also, his wife's grandfather was in her family's home. His grandfather had been kept between the walls for three years. Also, he had a small boy, a child of three months who died. Families were kept poor because of cremations. Moedra personally thought that it was a great waste of money to make such elaborate cremations, and thought it would be better to bury the dead instead of keeping them in the house until cremation time. Balinese wanted to be sure the body was cremated, so burying a body was uncertain as the body could be lost, and thereby would lose nirvana as well.

He also explained about the ecstasy of the Kriss Dance. He said the bad spirits were supposed to enter the dancer. As long as these bad spirits were in them, they could not feel, nor could they wound themselves with the sharp swords. When the bad spirits left them, they began to feel the blades and would stop torturing themselves. Priests also knew when to take the swords from them before they did themselves harm. Women also took part at times. Twice a year such a dance was held to celebrate the anniversary of the temple. The Balinese year was every six months. Each kampong desa temple had its own anniversary, so the Kriss Dances could be held any day in the year. Each kampong observed it twice a year.

Late at night, the four of us retired in one room. It stormed all night and we began to worry about the rivers rising. We left next morning at five thirty for Tukatbalian. Moedra went with us as far as Antasari so we walked back over the winding road we first came over when we arrived in Bali. It was beautiful and cool. We could hear and see the pounding surf, and see the isle of Java. We walked many kilometers. It began to rain.

We heard the bus coming. We hailed it and found Moedra sitting in front with the driver. He had asked the driver to leave three hours earlier than scheduled as it was pouring in Badjra he was afraid we would also be caught on the road in the storm. The bus took us to the big river Tukatbalian, and Moedra rode with us. It was raining hard. The bus had to remained on one side of the river and we three crossed over on a large, bamboo raft, which substituted for the former frail outrigger canoe. We saw the assistant "Resident of Negara," who was crossing in his own car. We walked to the shelter where we had slept before. It was now converted to a little restaurant and dwelling for the owner, who was the ferryman a few weeks ago. It continued to pour rain.

Joe hailed a resident motorist from the middle of the road, but the motorist tipped his hat and sped on, not even stopping to see what the matter was. In such weather, it was just downright meanness. Moedra could hardly speak, he felt so badly. One bus stood there empty. Even after Moedra spoke to him, the driver wanted fl 4 to take us five kilometers to Sebali River. The rain stopped, so we decided to walk it. Moedra had to return to Badjra. So again, we bade each other farewell. A Javanese boy went with us, all the way from Den Pasar carrying auto lacquer and paint for his taxi in Negara.

We hiked to the Selabi River where we found the Resident's empty car. He could not cross with it. There was no bus anywhere! So, we continued going, crossing the river over the newly-placed rocks and wire. We continued, with the young boy, for about four kilometers. There, at a native restaurant, we found the Resident pacing back and forth impatiently. He excused himself and told us he had thought we were going to Den Pasar when we hailed him. He had sent natives ahead on foot to get a bus or car to fetch him. He had a lovely Javanese woman with him — beautifully dressed in native costume and costly jewelry. We never learned the Resident's name.

The bus came and was filled with natives, baskets, and wares. Like the Kaiser himself, the Resident loudly and domineeringly ordered the natives off the bus. He told the bus to turn around and take him and the Javanese woman to Pulukan River. It was a nasty action. He could have let the bus continue the few kilometers with the native passengers, and then come back to fetch him. The Resident knew we wanted to get to Negara on time to take the outrigger, so he told us to get on the bus, and we rode up to Pulukan where another bus, loaded with copra, stood by.

We got to the pasangrahan before noon. There was a note for us from Kane: "The outrigger would be sailing today. I will try to hold them until one P.M." We took a car and rushed only to find that they had already sailed. There was another note from Kane, "A storm tide was in, and all outriggers had left that morning at nine A.M." No outriggers would sail for three days because it was the Javanese New Year.

We went back to the pasangrahan. The Javanese caretaker told us that we might be able to sail out in two days, as two other couples had ordered an outrigger for that day. They had also reserved two rooms at the pasangrahan. We might have had to find other quarters if the Resident had remained, but since he had left, there was room for us. At three P.M. the Dutch and Danish couples arrived.

We became acquainted, and found the Dane was a manager of a sugar cane plantation and factory. He and his wife had been here for twenty-two years. Because he was not a Dutchman, he was discriminated against and had lost his job because the sugar cane factories were shutting down. He was over forty-five years old, and it was impossible for him to get another job in Java. They must return to Europe or go to America where he had a sister.

They told us how the Dutch exploited the Javanese by renting their lands to the natives on contract for twenty-one years. But, due to bad sugar markets, they stopped growing sugar cane and canceled their contracts with the natives with no compensation. The natives could do nothing. The Dutch had violated their agreement, and did what they wished.

We stayed at the pasangrahan for two nights. We were invited to take the outrigger with the two couples. We left in a taxi at seven thirty. The outrigger, Buitenzarg, was just coming ashore with an Arab couple on board. We left the shore at nine for Banjuwangi, Java. If these people had not ordered this craft, we would have had to wait another day and night. Because of the holiday no outriggers had been regularly scheduled.

Perhaps Bali will be the last place we can find real beauty. So, I thanked the gods of Bali and of Olympus for keeping Bali for us this long, until we had a glimpse of the last little bit of Paradise remaining on Earth.

As a whole, the voyage was fine. At first the outrigger advanced slowly, as there was no wind. Both Malay boatmen rowed hard for an hour. We skirted closely the Bali coast. A few palm-bamboo huts could be seen through the trees close to the beach. Thick vegetation grew up to the black-sand beach. Coco palms waved above the tree line. It was hot, and the glare from the water was painful even though clouds hid the sun.

Each time the wind died one oarsman would tap the boat in a tattoo and whistle in a peculiar way. He was calling the wind to come and push us. Time and time again he did this in all seriousness. Actually calling on the wind! And the wind always came out of the calm, as if by a miracle, to carry the outrigger swiftly over the water. We put up the palm roof to avoid the scorching sun. Then a dead calm came again where nothing moved. Even the hard rowing of the boatmen seemed to do us no good. One remarked that we would have to spend the night on the water if no wind came before the tides went out. We couldn't get to shore by rowing against the tide. Rain came to make our waiting a little more unpleasant. The roof leaked. The deck was running with water, and we had to move around continually. We realized how powerless a sailboat was at the mercy of the winds. An hour or so of waiting brought wind and driving rain. The boatmen used the sail to every advantage with the wind and by rowing. The wind carried us across to the Java coast, but we were much out of our way. We came very close to the beach, and the boatmen rowed all the way into the harbor of Banjuwangi. It was a long and stiff pull.

One of our boatmen did not appear to be Javanese. He had one eye, but he closed it in such a way that one hardly realized it. He was a serene and proud-looking man and did not speak a word during the voyage. Nor did he drink or eat as his companion did. Smoking now and then, was the only diversion he allowed himself. From the time we left Tjupel until we arrive in Banjuwangi, he just paddled and watched the sail like a hawk. We had to respect him. These two boatmen had sailed from Banjuwangi the night before where three other outriggers had started also, but they had turned back due to bad weather. The Buitenzarg came across as it had been ordered. The Boatmen paddled and sailed all night with no sleep, and then went right back again, with us, to Java without even an hour's rest. We bade good-bye to the two couples and went our way.

Those people, in this outrigger, having lived in Java ten to twenty years, actually knew little of the Javanese or their country. It seemed to us they were disinterested, and took for granted what they heard from other residents and friends. Information we received from many people throughout Java proved to be wrong as we learned from our own experiences with the Javanese people. They looked down on the native, ridiculed him, and exploited him.

Madura

From Ujung, on the north shore of Java, we took a short crossing to Madura in a small steamboat. Trees and houses were discernible. Beautiful contrasts were made between the vivid tropic green and the red tile roofs of the Madura houses.

We landed at Kamal where there was a railroad depot and a bus depot at the landing. The trip took less than half an hour and the crossing reminded us of a trip we had taken on San Francisco Bay.

We strolled around the village located on a swampy beach, which had a terrible smell at low tide. Here too, were boats being decorated, repaired and built. The small houses were set low and made of woven bamboo with whitewashed sides and red tile roofs. All kind of scrap was used to build them. Although they were poor-looking and meager, there was an air of neatness and pride in these tiny houses. Each sat along the road overlooking the swampy beach.

There was a small pasar near the railroad depot. We spent half an hour trying to snap a photo of some of the women who were wearing huge bulky anklets. Nearly every woman wore these ornaments along with many silver or gold hair pins, and often fresh flowers were woven into the hair knot in back. They carried loads on their heads like the Balinese women. They dressed as the Javanese only they bunched their sarong in front into a big wad instead of folding it. This made them look pregnant.

The men were wilder-looking than the Javanese. They wore wide black trousers that reached half-way between the knees and ankles. They wore brilliant batik scarves, flowered jackets of thin material, and headdresses of batik squares tied roughly around the top exposing unruly hair. They liked brilliant colors. A Javanese looked prim, neat, and conservative, with neat sarong, military jacket, watch chain, sandals, orderly cap, smoked glasses and a briefcase. By comparison, the Madurese seemed freer, jollier and more akin to the Balinese in some ways. Most of the small children went naked.

Ridiculous looking carts were used in Madura. They were about four feet high. The floor was the seat for the driver and passengers who had to sit cross-legged. Beneath, were two beautifully-carved springs which held the cart to the axle. A basket filled with grass swung behind. This was food for the horse, no doubt. Some of these carts carried four passengers and had no back rail. Others were much longer and were enclosed like a box. When they went fast, the carts swayed from side to side on their flexible springs, and we thought any moment they would turn over. There were the usual little dog carts that were all over Java as well. But, these special Madurese carts seemed to be used more. The horse carts went faster, and the people rode in them in preference to the slower ones. All the ponies had feather dusters attached to the bridle above their heads. These looked comical when the horse began to trot bobbing up and down, in a ridiculous fashion.

The baby girls wore silver-colored metal anklets and bracelets like their mothers. They wore many more ornaments than the Javanese children. Their hats were cone-shaped, coming down well over the eyes, with a string tied under the chin.

Back at the bus depot, we spoke with two Malay boys who were working in the railroad depot. We asked them which nearby places in Madura were worth visiting. They thought it was novel thing that two Americans should bother to come to them for information. We then took a bus that was bound for the town of Bangkalan, about eighteen kilometers away. The bus driver and the ticket collector were jolly and kind. Two classes of passengers were designated on the bus. as there was only a few cents difference. This was a regular passenger bus with no baskets or cargo so we went first-class, for a change, The country looked flat and dry. The few rice fields were not pleasant to see. At regular intervals along the road, we saw small, raised shelters which held a hanging Malay time-drum. The drum was a hollowed log some three-and-a-half feet long, suspended by a rope. In some sections of the country, especially far away from the towns, the time of day was told by beating the drum, which had a far-reaching resonance. We saw similar kinds in Bali but they were always in a temple square.

Bangkalan consisted of one long main street lined with sleepy shops, owned by Malays and Chinese. One shop after the other had glass cases on the floor filled with the anklets, bracelets, chains and hair pins for the Madurese women. We were curious, so we went to one of the cases and asked the Chinese merchant to show us his wares. He knew we were just curious, but he kindly showed us a couple pairs of anklets. We were astounded at the weight. Some weighed as much as ten pounds. He showed us the metal bars from which they were made. I think it was a mixture of silver and lead.

The village was very hot. The asphalt pavement seemed to be melting, and the whitewashed stores gave off more glare. Most of the stores had large shades drawn down the front which made them look as if they were closed.

A canal ran through the city. We watched three men fishing under the main bridge. The water came to their waists. Together they pulled a large net against the current. As they caught a fish, they knocked it in the head. It was a filthy place to wade and to fish. The water muddy stank, as the canal was filled with much refuse.

We were hungry and tired, and the local Madurese restaurant had nothing to offer us. I took a plate of rice and tried some sort of meat and sauce but had to return it after one taste. So, the woman brought me one of those famous duck eggs that seem to be rotten but are not; they are only salty. She was not offended because we couldn't eat her food.

Nearly all of the women and young girls had fragrant flowers woven into their hair. There was no religious significance to it as there was in Bali, where only when going to the temple do the Balinese women wear flowers which had been blessed by the priest.

We spent only a few hours in Bangkalan. When we tried to get to another town, we found there were no buses, and the trip was too far for dogcart. As we waited for the bus returning to Kamal, we watched a cold-drink vendor in front of us. His stand consisted of two compartmentalized boxes which hung from either end of a pole. He carried his shop on his shoulder. One box held a glass jar of vivid pink fruit flavoring which was thick with sugar. Another glass jar had coconut milk with pieces of shredded coconut. He had two glasses, a dipper, a few bamboo sticks, and a small enameled spoon. To make a glass of ice-cold drink, he took his little bit of ice and rubbed it over a grater which was built on his stand. Then he poured a spoonful of the red syrup over the ice, and filled the glass with the coconut milk. He received one penny for it.

A small boy came by and gave his order. The vendor took a small Chinese tea bowl, held it under the shredder, and rubbed his ice over it. When the bowl was full, he took a little bamboo stick and thrust it into the ice. Then he pressed it into shape, so it would be firm. The whole thing came out of the bowl as a nice ball — like a popsicle. He then poured a spoon of the red syrup over it, received his penny, and the little boy walked off happy with his purchase.

We took the boat back to Ujung, and a train to Surabaya. It had rained most of the day in Surabaya, but because of certain wind currents we had had no rain in Madura. We stayed five days in that hot box of Surabaya, making our preparations for our passage to Saigon. We had to get health certificates and our Dutch entrance fee deposit back. We bought cots and a blanket, had my shoes soled, and bought a new pair of tennis shoes, since I had practically worn out my walking shoes in Bali.

Finally, on the 15th of February, 1932, at one thirty P.M., we piled into a taxi and raced down to the docks. It was hard to find the boat because she was so small and she was hidden by big molasses tanks. Our driver drove back and forth trying to find it, and then it began to rain in torrents. We finally found the Piquet and boarded her during a tropical cloudburst. There was noone to welcome us aboard since we boarded as deck passengers. In fact, there was no deck visible at all. It was piled with coal cinders and ash, and the whole deck was a few inches deep with water. Nobody was there to tell us where we belonged. It was a cold, wet beginning.

Of all the tiny, filthy boats that have ever left a trail of black smoke on the blue waters of the tropical seas, the rusty little Piquet took the prize. It ran between the Dutch East Indies and Saigon. All the coal ashes from the boilers were dumped on the deck, damming up the rainwater and causing the mess. On this antiquated tub, the ashes had to be carried out by hand from below in old kerosene cans that were hoisted up on a dumb waiter. At one end of the boat was a hand pump for fresh water. The French-Indo Chinese deck hands went in continuous procession carrying five-gallon tins of water to all parts of this tub. What space there was in the bow and stern of the boat was filled with big drums of tar.

There were barely any accommodations for passengers. If it stormed, which happened every day in these parts, we had to huddle in the tiny salon that reeked of old age and mildew, and was just big enough to turn around in. The decks were black with soot, cinders, rust, and the accumulations of general dirt that generally was absent on other boats. This boat also served as a blacksmith shop with a forge, a carpenter's wood-working shop, and a lathe and vise. In addition, this little tub flew the colors of the laundryman's fraternity — a long line of trousers, jackets, and undershirts which flew in the wind and the rain fore and aft.

Later on we saw a descriptive folder of this tub in a steamship office, put out by an agent for this line. It was a folder with apparently very old pictures… Ah! No folder could lure us again, no matter how rosy the colors. The folder would not have made a difference in our decision to take the Piquet. It was her route we wanted. But she did have a folder!

She was a cargo boat primarily, and she was French to boot. That is all that need be said. Her cleanliness was not evident. No woman had eyed the Piquet, or pointed out the corners of dirt and grime. I certainly would not want to shake the blissful composure of the Piquet's crew.

On our first night, the officers had their dinner in the little mess room. One member of the kitchen crew came with a large wooden board and sat himself in front of it on the deck, at the doorway of the mess room. He had taken a little stool only two inches high from its hiding-place and sat on it. He had a couple of towels a can of hot water, a dish mop, and a pot to gather the garbage. There he waited. Inside, one waiter served the officers, and as each officer finished his course, the dishes were whisked out to the waiting dishwasher, on his little stool, to be cleaned. The dumb waiter was connected to the kitchen on the poop deck. Lively conversations would issue from above and below, calling for clean dishes, warning that food was on its way down, etc. There seemed to be very few dishes in current circulation, therefore, the few in service had to do double duty. The little dishwasher was the funniest sight, as he sat on his two-inch stool waiting for dirty dishes to come out. It took a Chinese to have the patience, and sense and dignity, while doing the most insignificant work. Their seriousness made us smile.

A spellbound Chinese coolie watched me pound the typewriter. He could not see how the paper kept coming out by itself, and the roman letters were, of course, a puzzle to him. The deck was dark, and I could not see. Another one of Piquet's conveniences! I prayed it would not rain that night, as it did the night before.

The next morning, the ship became a great workshop. Wire cables were stretched over the decks, and we heard the sonorous sounds of scraping and grinding to remove rust from year's accumulation. The cables were like stiff, unwieldy snakes, and they took up the complete deck. We had to climb over and under, squirm in and out, and make ourselves small against the sides as we passed fore and aft.

I had wondered when the Piquet had had her last coat of paint. Rust had changed the white paint to brown, while dirt had made the brown turn black. Paint was an unknown factor on the hull of this boat.

The anvil resounded, and the bellows made an awful roar as sparks flew, and charcoal bits flew in the air. The shoveling of coal ash and cinders went on as usual on one side of the deck. The coolies carried the five-gallon cans of water that always leaked and left a trail of water behind them. The every day duties went on as usual, but we were just in the way, that's all. Before: I had called this ship a tub, but with all the activity that went on, it deserved a better title. Only the

Captain (the Omnipotent lord himself) had the luxury of privacy high up on his poop deck. He never showed himself, being of the caste of captains that puts himself above all deck hands and underlings. He was enormously fat, and to descend from his poop deck would have been, I fear, a most uncomfortable bit of exertion. I had not seen him as yet, although Joe had spoken with him in the agent's office and onboard a few days before we sailed out of Surabaya.

The sea was smooth as glass in the morning. In some places it was covered with a thin film of a brackish brown-colored substance, and in other places it was covered with a beautiful pea-green color. At first we thought it was mud from a river flowing to the sea, but we were far from land or any river. Our next thought was that it might have been a layer of volcanic ash blown in from somewhere, yet the vivid green color could not be ash. It might have been fine particles of organic sea matter floating on the surface and pieces of seaweed mixed with the fine layer.

Twice a day the Chinese coolies were fed. They sat on their haunches in a big circle, on the rusty foredeck, bowls in one hand against their mouths, and a pair of chopsticks in the other. In the center of the circle, on the deck a container held fish or meat for them. The chopsticks dove into the pot for meat, one after the other, and conveyed the morsels safely and accurately to the mouth. How they could shove in the mountains of rice! Somehow they kept up a continuous chattered and, never stopping an instant while eating. The two daily meals were thus devoured in haste and in obvious enjoyment.

I am convinced that the Chinese enjoy eating first of all, and then gambling. We observed that activity on the boat from San Francisco, then in China, and finally in the Dutch East Indies. Even the Chinese, who were born out of China, kept the Chinese ways. In our large Chinese hotel in Surabaya, the owner and his friends did little else but order food from fine Chinese restaurants, and play ma-jong and other games with high stakes. We had gone to sleep in the late hours to the sound of chips and excited voices, and then awakened at six or so in the morning to hear them still playing. A great pile of dishes, stacked on the outside steps, was evidence of their capacity for eating. Even on the Piquet, the Chinese stewards and deck hands gambled during leisure time — night and day — probably staking their next month's pay check, and maybe the one after that.

On board, we found a place for our cots on one side under a protected section of the deck. Sleeping was pleasant for the most part. Sometimes, a strong wind blew down the passageway, but we had fair protection from the rain. In the morning we used the officers' bath for bathing.

At first, we had a cold relationship with the officers but this wore off in time as we became acquainted. The first officer became friendly, and invited Joe to his cabin. Joe remained until midnight one evening while the officer told him about France, Indio-China, and the French Foreign Legion. The members of the legion, Joe was told, seemingly ceased to be humans any longer. The legion was made up of the worst of the French, German, and Spanish men — that is, those who were escaped convicts, refugees, and generally bad characters. The French government used them for keeping the native rebellions under control. They were a unique and terrible group and thought nothing of taking human lives. No other country had such a military group, but men from many nationalities joined it, and the French government felt they got better results from this mixed group than with units of all Frenchmen. In all the French colonies, there were about 5,000 men in the Foreign Legion. In Indo-China, there were about 2,000 Legionnaires.

In June 1931, there was a large uprising in North Indo-China. Some 2,000 natives demanded the French to leave. Forty Legionnaires, with the help of the French Air Force killed every one of the natives. After that, when a native saw a "red cap" or Legionnaire coming his way, he ducked in fear. The French, like all colonizers, were merciless it seemed.

The first officer, who was the first engineer, was a bachelor, of about 50 or 55 years of age. He had been on the sea for twenty-five years and was a comical-looking man with a gross figure, but he was good-hearted and kind. He was happy over the downfall of England as a world power. But he could not forget the grievances he still held against England from the Napoleonic times. He was an ardent reader of all good literature of every nation and was glad to speak with Joe, and exchange thoughts with one who had read the same books and could speak his language.

As a Frenchmen, he was a strong patriot and hated the Germans. The S. S. Piquet was a former German mine carrier built in 1914. There were big round doors and special chambers to bring cool air down the hatches where mines had been stored. After the war, the ship was taken from the Germans and given to France. It was well built and had an excellent engine. The officers told us about this with great satisfaction and irony.

Because of general world depression and a big drop in shipping, the shipping companies, like all other businesses, were losing money. So, the Piquet had to sail the seas devoid of paint or repairs. No cargo meant no money. It cost a lot to paint a ship and keep it clean and beautiful. The crews were reduced, as were the wages, and many ships were discontinued and anchored in the harbors.

Soon we reached Palembang. That was our second visit there and we saw that the river was a bee-hive of traffic as it was before. Oil refineries, coal yards, and river traffic combined to make this a heavy industrial center. But, this activity seemed insignificant compared to the immensity of the jungle and the river. The vast space this river occupied was remarkable.

The Chinese had chartered small steamers or paddle wheel boats decorated with red wreaths, banners, Dutch and Chinese flags, bunting, and greenery. Large signs in Chinese characters were also tacked on. We thought it was in honor of the Chinese New Year which had lasted a week or more already. But, we learned it was in honor of the Chinese victory over the Japanese in Shanghai. The Chinese here were as patriotic as those in China. They were as clannish as Jews in a strange land, and they were in touch with what was happening in their country. They read Chinese newspapers, and sent their children to special schools that taught the Chinese tongue in pure Mandarin. Those same neat, white-jacketed, Chinese shop keepers sent their boys to Java, or Singapore, or even to China to carry on and to be proud of the old traditions of China. A remarkable people, these Chinese!

For two whole days we had been in Palambang this time. We would not have thought we would be there a second time, but time plays strange twists, and there we were. However, it was not much out of the way, as we were bound for Saigon in French Indo-China. With good weather we planned to be there Monday afternoon.

We took passage on a large ship with a cargo of coal, so the ship rode smoothly. The voyage from Surabaya was beautiful. Of course, there had been much rain but that was to be expected in the tropics. We were used to rain and thought nothing of an occasional soaking. We dried off quickly anyway, and as we had nothing that could be ruined, we had nothing to lose from a soaking. These downpours usually came in the late afternoon and cooled things off. They resulted in gorgeous sunsets with golden rainbows arching the sky.

There were not really riverbanks here; it was just as if the Musi was a cleared portion of the jungle which was filled with water. Trees hung over the banks and the water extended far back into the jungle vegetation. The sight was most impressive, because here we felt the presence of virgin jungle and an unseen pulsing life hidden within. It was here we sensed the final supremacy of the powerful forces of nature and the struggles to overcome it.

The real Palembang, and the largest part of it, was the native section. There were no streets, so there was no way we could see the town by walking. The streets were water, and the Musi was Main Street. A double row of buildings four or five feet above the water made a "street." The "streets" extended only six or seven huts from the river. Even the jungle dared to defy Palembang. So, if you wanted to see the town, the best way to do it was from a native sampan.

Palm-roofed sampans, as well as big and little houseboats, served as dwellings for families. Just as we saw in Canton, the boats were a riot of colors. The natives piled their purchases neatly on the floor of the canoe. Their usually large straw rain-hats were put over their purchases to protect them from the sun or a sudden hard rain. Their wants were few, but it was important to them to have a river-worthy craft.

Sumatra was heavily forested and the soil was fertile. Its climate was wet and it rained frequently through the year. Rhinoceros, tigers, elephants, panthers, orangutans, and tapirs, were a few of the animals which lived there. The vegetable growth was more abundant than that of Java. The greatest source and variety of forest lumber in the Dutch islands came from here, producing gum and resins of great commercial value, such as camphor, pepper, and cinnamon.

There were many two-decked river boats propelled by large paddle wheels. They looked comical as they plied the river packed with passengers singing and shouting making it a festive party. The only other motor craft on the Musi were a few swift motor launches belonging to the Dutch companies and the government. The K.P.M. also had a few small steamers which plied the upper reaches of the Musi. They sailed mainly for government inspection work, but also carried passengers.

Palembang, like other towns in the Dutch East Indies, had many Chinese residents. They were of two classes, the majority middle-class and rich merchants, and a small colony of coolies. Coolies were somewhat rare in these parts, but we saw them as they came aboard the Piquet. They worked as laborers on the coaling ships shoveling coal. This was the first time we had seen coolies since we left Singapore.

On the S.S. Piquet, the crew was Indo-Chinese, some from Annam and some from Tonkin. The First Lieutenant was Cochin-Chinese, and the radio operator was from Tonkin. The First Lieutenant was a beautiful young man with a small nose, and rounded eyes. He carried himself proudly. He took Joe into his confidence and told him about their feelings against the French. It was mainly fear of the French brutality that kept them from revolting. There were many secret societies working in the country. It was said there were three leaders in Chochin-China who were very much like Gandhi, but not as famous as he was. The First Lieutenant asked Joe not to mention a word of what he had said to the French officers. Otherwise, he would lose his position immediately. Many papers and magazines were published in Indo-China but all were first censored by the French.

We set sail. The engines beat with the regularity of a clock, and with every turn of the propeller we advanced on our way. We laid on our deck chairs, very lightly dressed, and enjoyed the possibility of not being disturbed. What a delicious consciousness! No mail carrier could reach us, no telephone could annoy us, and in the next port there was nothing waiting for us. The flight from "everyday" had finally succeeded. We did not travel in order to arrive, but merely to travel. We quietly and lazily gazed upon the wide and glittering ocean for hours. The ocean waves murmured and beat day and night, and sea gulls accompanied the ship. For days we dreamed in the sunshine. The day began and ended with regularity and punctuality. We glided and rolled from one place to the next with no effort. However at every port, an invasion of merchants and hucksters came on board like a swarm of hornets.

The days passed, carefree, quietly and regularly — one exactly like the other. Objects and experiences behind us seemed to swim, disappear, and were swallowed by the endless lines of waves. The only reality remaining was the small world of the ship. And behind us, was the steaming jungle of a most unique land, peopled by a kind and generous, simple people whom we would long remember.

(*Journals were set aside during the leisurely sail from Sumatra to Saigon. on February 1932, they sailed toward Saigon*)

Addendum

Federal Malay States

The first European power to establish its influence in the Malay Archipelago was Portugal in 1497 occupying Malacca, Ternate, and Ambon. The first successful Dutch expedition was recorded in 1598. Soon after, the English established themselves in Batavia, Macassar, and Moluccas, Java (1811-16), and other parts of East Indies, under Sir Raffles.

The whole of the East Indies was restored to the Dutch after Napoleon's down-fall, on a reciprocal basis, with Holland ceding to Great Britain, all of her establishments on Continental India, the Island of Ceylon, and the town of Malacca.

The Federated Malay States were a very rich country full of valuable mineral deposits. It was like a luxurious garden which, when tickled, laughs itself into harvest. It seemed to be the only British colony where there was no unrest. The land of the Pruhu, or the treacherous Malayan people, had become a quiet "middle of the world" with a riot of vegetation down to the shore. Here, one finds fishermen's picturesque little bamboo huts underneath the coconut palms.

Bali culture

The population of Bali, was a Hindu-Javanese tribe, and within the Malayan race, a remarkable group on its own with distinct religion, morals, and culture. In the beginning of the 16th century numerous Javanese came to Bali to introduce Hinduism. The Islam faith was then predominant in Java, but did not get a firm foothold in Bali. This caused a rigid barrier between the two islands, and consequently, the cultural development of Bali went its own way.

Bali was not only a marvelously beautiful island, but it also had a unique culture entirely its own. The Balinese, inspired by their religious conviction, gradually acquired a near perfect skill in temple building. Magnificent temples were found throughout the island. Thus passed the beautifully decorated places, richly adorned with ingenious shapes and artistic forms. They mostly made use of sandstone, which was a soft material that moldered away rather quickly. This is why temples decayed and were constantly in need of renewal. Many new temples were being erected.

Bali, most probably, contained the purest strain of Javanese stock. The other islands, merged with other races. The Balinese men, for instance, were nearly a head taller than the Javanese, and were more muscular and enterprising. The women had radiant beauty and aristocratic refinement not to be found elsewhere in all the Indies.

Hinduism was very humane, and the sacrifices were mostly inanimate or floral. They partook far more in sacred thank-offerings than that of the Semitic idea of sacrifices of blood. The Hindu faith had left its mark in many temples, and statues of the Hindu gods were found everywhere on the island. And an even older faith, found alike from Japan to the Punjab, had given Bali its so-called *Merua*, the many-roofed pagoda-like structures that were memorials to the great dead, giving an air of infinite grace and beauty to the otherwise stagnant temples of Bali.

All of nature was the object of worship for the Animists; and in Bali, no exception was found to this general rule. The mountains, especially the *Gunoong Agoong* and the *Gunoong Batu Kau*, were held in special veneration, supposedly as places of residence of the gods. Temples and special shrines erected to various lakes, trees, caves, great rocks, hills, mountains and so on, in all parts of the island, were held in veneration. It was into this basic animism that the Hindu religion had been grafted and flourished.

As in all countries of the world, it was the common people who were the most interesting part of the community. In Bali, the men and women, for the most part enjoyed life in the most innocent ways imaginable. The Balinese pastimes most given to were dancing, music playing, and comedy acting, but cock fighting was still the most popular attraction.

The Balinese people were very industrious, and cultivated the finest systems of irrigated rice fields in the world. They bred a fine line of cattle and pigs. In the household industry, they produced fine metalwork in gold, silver and copper as well as woven goods with ornamented gold and silver thread. A very fine textile work called Prada work consisted of appliqué in gold and silver leaf on silk.

The recreation of the common people consisted largely of attending temple festivals, after which solemn celebrations and presentations of offerings, became a ceremonial picnic. At these gatherings, the wonderful Balinese dancers and actors performed. However these gatherings also offered the opportunity for staging cockfights.

One of the striking customs in Bali was the cremation ceremony, and the proceeding procession, which took place in a very solemn and stately manner. The government had abolished the former barbaric custom of widows perishing on the corpses of their husbands. The last cremation of this form took place at Tobanan in 1903 when the widow of the Rajah of Tobanan was burned alive.

The aristocratic Balinese was embalmed after his death. The poor could not afford that, but whatever his rank or caste, he was ultimately cremated. This was regarded literally as his key to paradise. These cremations were highly ceremonial simple or elaborate, according to the wealth of the person being cremated. In order to make the cremations of the poorer classes more fitting, it was the custom for people to band together and wait until there were from ten to one hundred of their dead ready for cremation, and then they had a great communal ceremony for them all.

The belief of the Balinese was that after cremation, the soul descended to earth in the form of mist, and in reincarnation is endowed with greater gifts. The soul would be regenerated seven times before it reached perfection and admitted into heaven — the realm of the supreme god, Shiva.

Cremation seldom happened immediately after death. Expenses were high and took time to arrange. Younger persons could not be cremated before elder members of the family. Therefore, cremation affected the entire family. Pending cremation, the dead either were buried or placed in some sort of a building. Higher classes were often embalmed while waiting. Brahman priests were consulted as to what day was best for cremation. The phase of the moon also played a role in their decisions. Great ceremonies developed for the cremation. Ceremonial towers were built and big feasts were held. Live chickens were supposed to play a part in carrying the souls of the departed. The remaining ashes were collected by the family and taken to the nearest river. The ashes then would be transmitted to the sea eventually, and so all remains would be vanished from the earth. Otherwise, regeneration would be impossible.

Religion of the Bali People

In Bali, as in Europe, the social affairs of the Balinese were guided and controlled by religious beliefs. Their beliefs were a curious mixture of Hinduism and Buddhism. The religion of the other islands in Dutch East Indies was either Mohammedan or ancient worship of deities and demons. On Bali, the religion was purely Hindu in origin. The cause of this was probably when the Arabs came to Java centuries ago, they forced Mohammedanism on the people at the point of a sword. Many, however, escaped and fled to Bali and adhered to Brahmanism or Hinduism. Here they established their culture and religion and successfully defended themselves against Moslem aggression. The Hinduism of Bali was in many ways purer, but more primitive than that of British India. It was the life of the people, and in their daily lives they live their religion. Nothing was done without the sanction of the priest, who was called to function on every possible occasion. But the Hindu priest, the Pandanda, was of lesser importance to the people. The Desa priest had more than a trace of animistic belief and ritual performed in his functions.

The caste system on Bali was not as hydra-headed as it was in India. There were four main castes. The Triwangsa caste, or Nobility caste, which was divided into three— Brahmans, Vesyas, and Satrias, but the great mass of common people were Sudras. Bali boasted a century of artist.

(Endnotes)

1. Mentok is current spelling. In 1932 it was Muntok
2. What we would consider a Bed and Breakfast accommodation
3. Pasar is an open market. This is the common market for all the villages visited.
4. Sampans are row boats of different sizes. Some used as a dwelling. Some used as a floating store. They are the primary means of local travel in the villages along the rivers.
5. Merak was spelled Murak in 1932. The spelling of many villages and towns were changed from the Dutch
6. On current maps of this Dutch controlled Indonesia the spelling of villages and towns have changed the Dutch spelling of the time in 1932 from "oe" to "u". This town was spelled Pramboemoelih. The editor has changed the spelling to current usage for those who wish to find the location on current maps of the islands.
7. Kompong: Small village settlement
8. Wajang is a "shadow puppet show"

Would you like to see your manuscript become a book?

CPSIA information can be obtained at www.ICGtesting.com
Printed in the USA
243263LV00002B/60/P

9 781462 617814